FUTURE-FOCUSED
LEADERSHIP

PREPARING SCHOOLS, STUDENTS, AND COMMUNITIES FOR TOMORROW'S REALITIES

GARY MARX

Association for Supervision and Curriculum Development • Alexandria, Virginia USA

Association for Supervision and Curriculum Development
1703 N. Beauregard St. • Alexandria, VA 22311-1714 USA
Phone: 800-933-2723 or 703-578-9600 • Fax: 703-575-5400
Web site: www.ascd.org • E-mail: member@ascd.org
Author guidelines: www.ascd.org/write

Gene R. Carter, *Executive Director*; Nancy Modrak, *Director of Publishing*; Julie Houtz, *Director of Book Editing & Production*; Ernesto Yermoli, *Project Manager*; Georgia Park, *Senior Graphic Designer*; Jim Beals, *Typesetter*; Dina Murray Seamon, *Production Specialist*

All Web links in this book are correct as of the publication date below but may have become inactive or otherwise modified since that time. If you notice a deactivated or changed link, please e-mail books@ascd.org with the words "Link Update" in the subject line. In your message, please specify the Web link, the book title, and the page number on which the link appears.

PAPERBACK ISBN-13: 978-1-4166-0219-4 ASCD product #105009   s1/06

PAPERBACK ISBN-10: 1-4166-0219-4

e-book editions: retail PDF ISBN-13: 978-1-4166-0350-4; retail PDF ISBN-10: 1-4166-0350-6 • netLibrary ISBN-13: 978-1-4166-0348-1; netLibrary ISBN-10: 1-4166-0348-4 • ebrary ISBN-13: 978-1-4166-0349-8; ebrary ISBN-10: 1-4166-0349-2.

Quantity discounts for the paperback edition only: 10–49 copies, 10%; 50+ copies, 15%; for 500 or more copies, call 800-933-2723, ext. 5634, or 703-575-5634. For desk copies: member@ascd.org.

Library of Congress Cataloging-in-Publication Data

Marx, Gary.
  Future-focused leadership : preparing schools, students, and communities for tomorrow's realities / Gary Marx.
     p. cm.
  Includes bibliographical references and index.
  ISBN-13: 978-1-4166-0219-4 (alk. paper)
  ISBN-10: 1-4166-0219-4 (alk. paper)
  1. Educational leadership. 2. School management and organization. 3. Leadership. I. Title.
  LB2805.M2843 2006
  371.2--dc22
                              2005027511

12 11 10 09 08 07 06   12 11 10 9 8 7 6 5 4 3 2 1

FUTURE-FOCUSED
LEADERSHIP

Acknowledgments

Future-Focused Leadership: Preparing Schools, Students, and Communities for Tomorrow's Realities is a gift that I hope will keep on giving. It is based on the premise that people can come together to create and constantly re-create an even better future for our schools, education systems, and the whole of society. In that spirit, dozens, if not hundreds, of thoughtful professionals in numerous fields joined the team that resulted in this publication.

First, my thanks to the Creating a Future Council of Advisors. The council of 34 individuals is listed at the end of these acknowledgments. They responded to either one or two questionnaires, helping me identify, sort, and expand on issues and trends. On top of that, they provided insights on the leader's role as generalist.

Second, I am grateful to the Educational Research Service. We worked together in 1999 to develop an ERS Schools of the Future Council. ERS then published my book *Ten Trends: Educating Children for a Profoundly Different Future* in 2000. That book has drawn significant attention to the need for educators to consider the implications of trends for their education systems and their students.

Third, I appreciate the thinking and inspiration of numerous World Future Society colleagues who are constantly stretching my thinking—people such as Marvin Cetron; Joseph Coates; Edward Cornish; Jeff Cornish; Susan Echard; Tim Mack; John Meagher; Graham T. T. Molitor; James Morrison; John Petersen; Herb Rubenstein; Rick Smyre; David Pearce Snyder; Edie Weiner; and Clem Bezold, Marsha Rhea, and Bill Rowley of the Institute for Alternative Futures, to name just a few. Some served as members of the advisory council.

Of course, many others provided information and ideas through their writings and research. The many professionals who work each day with the U.S. Census Bureau, the Social Security Administration, and the Bureau of Labor Statistics provide ongoing sets of data that help create a snapshot of who and where we are today and the direction we might be headed.

As a speaker and workshop leader in many parts of the United States and other parts of the world, I have gained inspiration and ideas that have enriched this book. The Pennsylvania School Boards Association, the Association of California School Administrators, the Bloomfield Hills Public Schools in Michigan, and Conciencia Argentina are among the many groups that have recently generated ideas that influenced this publication.

My deepest appreciation goes to the Association for Supervision and Curriculum Development (ASCD), the publisher of this book. Scott Willis, Nancy Modrak, Doug Soffer, Ernesto Yermoli, and Kathleen Florio have been particularly encouraging and helpful. Kathleen Burke took an early interest in my futures work, even before joining the ASCD staff. ASCD Executive Director Gene Carter has been a longtime mentor and colleague whose openness to ideas and commitment to sound education combine to provide the type of leadership described in this book.

Special appreciation and admiration go to Judy Marx, an educator whose ideas, assistance, and encouragement have helped to make this book and my mission possible. I am especially grateful to my children, John and Daniel, whose intense interest in people and ideas is helping them blaze new trails in their professions.

Now I thank you, my readers, for turning words and ideas on a printed page into actions that will help create the education system of the future. I want you to read this book, use it as a reference, and get copies for others to stimulate their thinking about the future. Most of all, I'd like to have *Future-Focused Leadership: Preparing Schools, Students, and Communities for Tomorrow's Realities* serve as a launching pad, not a resting place. Your assignment is, as they say, to "run with it."

—Gary Marx

The Creating a Future Council of Advisors

Early in 2004, members of the Creating a Future Council of Advisors responded to either one or two rounds of questionnaires. In the first, advisors were asked to identify significant trends and issues that might affect education and society in the early part of the 21st century. In the second, they were asked to share what they considered the implications of a cluster of three trends and to comment on the importance of leaders capable of making connections in a complex, fast-moving world.

The views expressed in this publication do not necessarily reflect the beliefs or opinions of any member of the council or the council as a whole, nor do they reflect the official views of ASCD.

Members of the Council of Advisors are **Drew Albritten,** executive director, Council for Exceptional Children; **Kenneth Bird,** superintendent, The Westside Community Schools, Omaha, Nebraska; **Ted Blaesing,** superintendent of schools, White Bear Lake, Minnesota; **Carol Brown,** 2003–2004 president, the National School Boards Association; **Kimberley Cetron,** teacher, Fairfax County Public Schools, Virginia; **Marvin Cetron,** president, Forecasting International, Ltd., Falls Church, Virginia; **Joseph F. Coates,** president, Consulting Futurist, Inc., Washington, D.C.; **Kenneth Dragseth,** superintendent of schools, Edina, Minnesota, and 2003 National Superintendent of the Year; **Marc Ecker,** former president, the National Middle School Association, Westerville, Ohio, and superintendent of schools, Fountain Valley, California; **Arnold Fege,** president, Public Advocacy for Kids, Annandale, Virginia; **Douglas Greenberg,** president and CEO, the Survivors of the Shoah Visual History Foundation, Los Angeles, California; **Elizabeth L. Hale,** president, the Institute for Educational Leadership, Washington, D.C.; **Jane Hammond,** superintendent-in-residence, the Stupski Foundation, Mill Valley, California; **Linda Hodge,** 2003–2005 president, the National Parent-Teacher Association, Chicago, Illinois; **George Hollich,** former director of curriculum and summer programs, Milton Hershey School, Hershey, Pennsylvania; **David**

Hornbeck, former president and CEO, International Youth Foundation, Baltimore, Maryland, and currently president, Children's Defense Fund, Washington, D.C.; **John Hoyle,** professor of educational administration, Texas A&M University, College Station, Texas; **Ryan Hunter,** middle school student, Long Island, New York; **Rick Kaufman,** executive director, public engagement and communication, the Jefferson County Public Schools, Colorado, and 2003–2004 president, the National School Public Relations Association; **Keith Marty,** superintendent, School District of Menomonee Falls, Wisconsin; **Radwan Masmoudi,** founder and president, Center for the Study of Islam and Democracy, Washington, D.C.; **Frank Method,** director of education policy, the Research Triangle Institute, International, Washington, D.C.; **Graham T. T. Molitor,** president, Public Policy Forecasting, Potomac, Maryland, and vice president and legal counsel, the World Future Society, Bethesda, Maryland; **Bob Mooneyham,** executive director, the National Rural Education Association, Norman, Oklahoma; **Carol G. Peck,** president and CEO, Rodel Charitable Foundation, Scottsdale, Arizona; **James Rickabaugh,** superintendent, Whitefish Bay School District, Whitefish Bay, Wisconsin; **Betsy Rogers,** teacher, Jefferson County School System, Birmingham, Alabama, and 2003 National Teacher of the Year; **Gary Rowe,** president, Rowe Inc., Lawrenceville, Georgia; **Douglas Shiok,** superintendent, Orange North Supervisory Union (school district), Williamstown, Vermont; **Michael Silver,** superintendent-in-residence and visiting lecturer, University of Washington College of Education, Seattle, Washington, and currently assistant professor of education administration, Seattle University; **Rosa Smith,** president, Schott Foundation and Schott Center, Cambridge, Massachusetts; **David Pearce Snyder,** consulting futurist, The Snyder Family Enterprise, Bethesda, Maryland; **Ted Stilwill,** former director, Iowa Department of Education, Des Moines, Iowa, and president, Council of Chief State School Officers, Washington, D.C., currently director of learning, Iowa Environmental Project; and **V. Wayne Young,** executive director, the Kentucky Association of School Administrators, Frankfort, Kentucky.

Introduction

Change is inevitable. Progress is optional.

—*Anonymous*

Think about it: That energetic, inspired child who emerged from kindergarten in 2005 will graduate from high school in about 2017 and college in about 2021. That same student will likely celebrate a 90th birthday in 2090. Many members of the kindergarten class of 2005 will live beyond 2100, into the 22nd century. The average 2010 high school graduate will turn 65 in about 2057 and could confront 90 candles on a birthday cake in 2082. What's the conclusion here? The future is in school *today.*

None of us asked to be born at this time in history, but here we are. We are the first generations of people capable of destroying the world, and we may be the last generations who can save it. Much will depend on how we educate our people. Education is that important, and the future is coming at us at warp speed. There is no place to hide.

Forget the status quo. It has become a ticket to obsolescence. There is no more business as usual. We now realize that, in a fast-moving world, the organization, community, or country that unleashes the genius of its people through the best possible education will move forward at an unprecedented rate. Unfortunately, the organization, community, or country that does *not* unleash the genius of its people through the best possible education will fall backward at the same dizzying pace.

The challenge is clear. For anyone in any profession—but especially *all* educators—creating a future is the essence of leadership. None of us, nor our organizations, can be frozen in time. Instead, we need to see ourselves as works in progress. Unless we constantly lead the process for shaping a future, someone else will do it for us. The world will not stand still. It's that simple ... and that complex.

"But the agenda is already full," some people might point out. "How do you expect us to think about the future?" It's true that present-day issues are consuming. They can fill 24 hours a day, 7 days a week, 52 weeks a year. In fact, ask most educators about the issues they face and they will quickly list the following: federal and state requirements; high-stakes testing; achievement gaps; budget needs; staffing; disciplinary concerns; parent and community support; dealing with diversity; attracting and keeping a staff of highly qualified professionals; the condition of facilities; class size; attendance; the need to maintain, upgrade, and more effectively use technology; and a host of others.

Each of these issues is important, without a doubt. However, unless we can think beyond the top-of-the-desk issues of the day, the world will go around, over, or through us. We need to be constantly connected with the world outside our immediate system or discipline. If we aren't, then the organization itself will become isolated, out of touch, and incapable of preparing students for the future.

Some educators express legitimate concern about measuring up to state and federal requirements. "It's do or die," they say. "How can we pay attention to the future when the present is sucking up all our time?" Whatever the requirements, we simply must create a future on top of them. Otherwise, educators will be relegated to the status of compliant bureaucrats, waiting for the next set of instructions from a state or national capital.

One way educators can redirect their attention, given the blizzard of pressing issues of the day, is to add an ongoing challenge in the form of a question. Consider this: Students in the high school class of 2017 are now in school; they will be approximately 21 in 2021 and 65 in 2065. What are the implications for education?

Strategic Plan, Living Strategy, or Both?

Remember the line "The emperor has no clothes"? Here is something even more audacious: "The plan has no shelf life."

"How can that be?" some may ask. "Our vision and mission statements define us, and our goals and objectives focus on what we intend to do."

That's true, and it will likely be the case for a long time to come. The big change is that the plan—whether it is a district- or other organization-level strategic plan or an individual school improvement plan—cannot gather dust on a shelf. The plan needs to move from the top shelf to the top of the desk and become an ongoing agenda. The world is going through exponential transformation, and no one has a foot on the brake. That's why we need to be sure that our plan is flexible and supports any quick changes needed to help us deal with problems or opportunities that come at us out of the blue. It should promote a living strategy that stimulates creativity, imagination, and even audaciousness. It should be an enabling, not an inhibiting, piece of work. It should help us adjust and even become comfortable with complexity theory—an assumption that the landscape will be constantly changing, that we must thrive in a dynamic world of uncertainty and a diversity of players, issues, and trends.

The plan should not represent the end of a process. It should be the beginning of an adventure aimed at preparing our education system and our students for a fast-changing environment. The plan should, at best, be a window on the future, not a wall that holds us back from possibility.

A "living strategy" emerges and continuously evolves from "the collective knowledge of the community and from ongoing dialogue among all members of the community," according to Paul Borawski, executive director of the American Society for Quality, and Arian Ward, president,

CEO, and cofounder of Work Frontiers International. "It is critical to pay attention to the relationship between components," they say, because "small changes can have large effects." The plan, they explain, can help establish "a hoped-for direction" but may not be able to precisely describe "the ultimate goal" (Borawski & Ward, 2004, pp. 6–9, 12–13).

This book, and the processes it suggests, will help education systems— and any organization, for that matter—stay close to the rapidly evolving edge of opportunity. What it has to say is basic to establishing a living strategy and moving the plan from the shelf to the desk to an evolving agenda. It emphasizes the belief that what we need is a constantly changing, working, strategic guide on the pathway to a future that, today, just might be beyond our imaginations.

It's clear. We need a strategic plan—but we also need a living strategy.

How Big Is the Box?

"We need to get outside the box!" How many times have we heard that statement? How many times have we said it? Do we really mean it, or does this mantra simply state some seemingly unattainable dream?

Breaking through the tough inner and outer walls of organizational, philosophical, and even habitual boxes can be a formidable task, but it is also essential. So how can we penetrate the containers and form a constant, organic connection with the political, economic, social, technological, environmental, and other forces that are buffeting our communities and the planet? In short, how can we keep ourselves and our organizations in tune with the exponentially expanding needs, problems, and opportunities posed by the world around us?

Perhaps, if a box is necessary, we need to make it bigger, to encompass the emerging needs of people over space and time. Although we surely must be concerned about our personal, family, and community well-being, we must also realize that we ride together through space on a medium-sized planet that increasingly demands our attention. We have a great deal in common with people everywhere, including, at the most basic level, our survival.

By its very nature, education is not just for today. We are, indeed, preparing students to become well-adjusted, interested, and interesting people who are good citizens and employable. They will be the ones who will play a major role in determining whether we will even have a future and, if so, the kind of future it will be. That's big thinking, and that's how big and important education is to our individual and collective futures. The box is suddenly much more expansive, and its edges reach beyond the horizon. As R. Buckminster Fuller put it, "If it is true that the bigger the thinking becomes the more lastingly effective it is, we must ask, 'How big can we think?'" (1969, p. 59).

About This Book

In essence, this book is about the process of constantly creating a future. It addresses the premise—though not often stated directly—that any leader must be an environmentalist, adapting the organization to the needs of a fast-changing social environment and the environment to the needs of the organization.

While we are "reaching in" to nurture students and improve the effectiveness of the organization, we also need to be "reaching out," connecting with the exciting challenges that will greet us on the road to the future. If we don't, our highest aspirations for students, our compelling goals, and our hopes for the future might pull to a screeching halt. Anyone who reads this book from cover to cover and takes it to heart should understand the sense of urgency about making an organization more flexible—less static and more dynamic.

The book is based on the following assumptions:

- True leaders need to see the bigger picture, no matter how specialized and important their specific responsibilities are.

- Virtually all educators—teachers, administrators, and others—should see themselves as leaders because of the critical roles they play in society. In education, leadership goes with the territory.
- Educators should strive to be intellectual leaders, seeing ideas, events, and even disciplines in context, not floating in a sea of separateness.
- Educators need to be connected with the environment. They need to understand how to consider and even shape societal trends. Every educator should be adept at seeing the connection between education and massive political, economic, social, technological, environmental, demographic, and other forces that affect their personal lives, their schools, their communities, their countries, and the world.
- Although *content* is vital for effective education and leadership, it is *process*, driven by strategic communication, that pulls the expanding mass of knowledge into a coherent whole.
- Old, unsolved problems can accumulate and overtake us from generation to generation, inhibiting our ability to shape the organization to fit within an entirely new social landscape.
- Even those who have been rigid, who have found their refuge in the status quo, can find the process of continually shaping a future exciting, interesting, and downright fulfilling. Those who avoid the complexity will miss most of the fun.

This book assumes that you, the reader, know something about planning. Although it reviews processes that should be considered essential in developing a formal plan, it doesn't focus directly on how to develop a mission statement or sets of goals and objectives. Instead, it zeroes in on what might be called "reading the environment." That, of course, is one of the most essential steps in developing a vision for the future, in giving shape to the planning process, and in maintaining the flexibility to navigate the education system, or any other organization, through a world of exponential change.

Creating an Agenda for Action

This publication provides building blocks for staying in touch with trends and issues. It is designed to help you and your organization become poised for developing and renewing your vision. Staying ahead of the curve puts you in an even better position to take the initiative, to pursue a living strategy—an agenda for action.

Although the book emphasizes education, it can also be used by people in other fields; businesses; communities; governmental and nongovernmental organizations; associations, foundations, and professional societies; countries; and international organizations that want to prepare for the future. It is purposely written to provide stimulating reading, offer ready access to a broad range of data and information, promote discussion, contribute to planning, and serve as a text or subtext for courses on leadership, planning, future studies, or other topics.

A companion book, *16 Trends: Their Profound Impact on Our Future* (2005), published by the Educational Research Service, presents an in-depth analysis of far-reaching trends with often dramatic implications for education and for other organizations, institutions, and professions. A list of the 16 trends, found in Chapter 4 of this book, serves as a virtual table of contents for that publication.

I wish you happy and adventurous reading and an exciting future.

Questions

1. How would you define the difference between a strategic plan and a living strategy?
2. When will the current class of kindergartners in your local schools graduate from high school? When will they graduate from college? When will they turn 65?
3. Why is the status quo no longer a reasonable refuge?

Readings

Fuller, R. B. (1969). *Operating manual for spaceship Earth*. Carbondale, IL: Southern Illinois University Press.

PART 1

The future-capability of society . . . involves rethinking in the educational sector, above all among those doing the learning and teaching.

—*Rita Sussmuth (1998)*

The Connected Leader

Isolation is expensive. Why? Because the new coin of the realm is information and relationships. What we know and who we know both count. Unless we are firmly connected to those we depend on and those we serve, we will very likely lose touch, and that's something we can't afford to do.

Part 1 makes a case that leaders, to be successful, need to be connected generalists. It also presents 12 guiding principles for leaders who are capable of the continual process of creating a future.

1

The Leader as a Connected Generalist

Too many of today's organizations are over-managed and underled.

—*Warren Bennis (1998)*

We all know the story. With only a hammer and chisel, the carver is intent, masterfully shaping a stone. An onlooker asks, "What are you doing?" Stopping for a moment, the carver eagerly replies, "I'm building a cathedral." The carver could have said, "I'm chiseling a stone," "I'm making a gargoyle," or "I'm carving a stone for the west wall." This artisan knew the stone had to be masterfully carved, but he also knew it was part of something even more majestic.

At its best, education is majestic, touching every aspect of human endeavor. That pervasiveness means that educators who hope to prepare their schools and their students for the future must be connected to the complex, fast-moving world around them.

Pursuing this noble and never-ending goal will require all the visionary leadership we can muster. Leading the process of developing a constantly evolving vision for education won't be easy, but it's sure to be the most exciting and important thing we could ever do.

Insightful leaders in education are the first to admit that a 20th century system may not be adequate to prepare students for life in the 21st century. Change is tough, but change may be less of an issue than deciding what we need to become. What are the characteristics of an education system that will groom students—in our community, in our country, in the world—for life in a global knowledge/information age?

To get this ongoing process under way, most of us will need to change old habits. But, come to think about it, those old habits weren't much fun anyway. Rather than knowing all the answers, we'll likely discover the exhilaration of searching for the right questions. Richard Feynman, educator, winner of the 1965 Nobel Prize for Physics, and master of dealing with complexity, said, "I can live with doubt and uncertainty and not knowing. I think it is much more interesting to live not knowing than to have answers that might be wrong" (Beaty, 2004).

Leaders in the 21st century will need to be highly adept in their specialties. At the same time, they will be expected to be generalists, eager to connect a broad range of people and ideas. The successful ones will constantly and enthusiastically seek to build a connecting web in what is too often a vacuum between disciplines, and they'll enjoy every minute of it. In a fast-moving world, these thoughtful and exemplary leaders will wrest coherence from growing turbulence and complexity.

As generalists and as education leaders, they will help students learn across disciplines. They will constantly scan the environment, seeking opportunities to bridge the divides between bodies of knowledge, cultures, ideologies, languages, and political divisions. By poking their heads above the specialization of their industries, institutions, or professions, leaders in any field are in a better position to discover common threats, and, better yet, common opportunities.

The Expansion of Leadership

In the strictly vertical organization, the leader was often seen as a solitary figure at the top of the pyramid. Information went up; orders came down. Today, however, the vertical is becoming increasingly horizontal.

Knowledge is growing so rapidly that the person at the top cannot even pretend to know everything. Although those who provide central leadership for organizations require broad general knowledge and experience, they can survive and be effective only if they are surrounded by a team of people who also see both the big and little pictures.

"Information isn't in the hands of one person," says James Surowiecki in *The Wisdom of Crowds* (2004). "It's dispersed across many people. So relying only on your private information to make a decision guarantees that it will be less informed than it could be" (p. 51).

Surowiecki's observation provides all the more reason for leaders to be facilitators. According to Greg Madsen and Barry Rosen (1994) of Interaction Associates, facilitation involves coaching and serving as both a team leader and a change agent. Central to facilitative leadership is bringing out the best in others; developing and sharing an inspiring vision; modeling behaviors that lead to collaboration; focusing on results, process, and relationships; designing pathways to action; trying to achieve maximum appropriate involvement; and celebrating accomplishment.

In short, the concept of leadership has been expanded. Some would even say it has been dispersed. A board member, superintendent, college or university president, principal, or department head might have highly significant and sensitive executive and policymaking responsibilities. However, all understand that their success is dependent on the leadership of talented teachers and others who are part of the team. As leaders, educators need to appreciate the connection between their contributions inside and outside the classroom and their broader impact on society as a whole.

The 21st century leader is duty-bound to constantly encourage the creation of a future for the education system. Yesterday's system may not be able to address tomorrow's needs. That's why we need to perceive renewal and change as less threatening and more a part of how the system and everyone in it function. We are, after all, preparing our students for the future, not for the past. We're all in this together.

Understanding Our Interconnected World

The world is connected. Even with concerted effort, we would find it difficult to escape the effect of what seem like faraway events on our daily lives. Our access to information has increased exponentially. We've experienced firsthand the dizzying speed of communication and transportation that bring people and ideas closer together.

Access to Information

Millions, if not billions, of people now have ready access to information. In fact, we face a constant barrage of opportunities to make connections among vast arrays of ideas and facts—a privilege once available to only a few. Information is power, and for millennia some people hoarded it, parceling it out to fit their own autocratic interests. No more.

"Technology has been democratized," former NBC News president Larry Grossman (1998) reminded a World Future Society audience. "Printing made us all readers. Xeroxing made us all publishers. Television made us all viewers. Now digitization has made us all producers," he remarked.

Socially responsible leaders make every effort to stay close to those they serve—to determine their needs and figure out how to be of service. That effort is basic to the concept of servant leadership. Much of what we need to know is available by listening. Mohandas Gandhi suggested, "Look below the surface and identify the hidden and unarticulated needs that others cannot see, and create a bond with those you are trying to serve" (Nair, 1994, p. 83).

Speed of Communication and Transportation

The escalating stream of information and ideas necessary for broad-based enlightenment is being driven by the marriage of communications technology and computing. The integrated system, just a gleam in someone's eye a short time ago, has now become the Internet or the more contained intranet. Interactive technologies have shortened the lag time between action and reaction to microseconds. We can have nearly instant access to a world of information and experiences that burst across political and cultural boundaries.

Satellites, high-speed computers, and high-tech aircraft have shrunk the globe, while spacecraft have taken us beyond our home planet. In the 1700s and early 1800s, Thomas Jefferson lived in a four-mile-an-hour world. When Abraham Lincoln was assassinated in 1865, the news didn't hit London newspapers until 12 days later. With the transoceanic cable in place, accounts of the 1883 eruption of the volcano Krakatoa hit major newspapers the next day (Winchester, 2004). When, to our collective horror, the space shuttle *Columbia* disintegrated in 2003, we watched it live, in real time.

Complexity and Connection

Leaders in every field must be ready to consider a broad range of political, economic, social, technological, environmental, and other forces as they make decisions about what to say and what to do. For educators, those implications expand to include what to teach and how to teach it. Educators and their students—and everyone else, for that matter—simply must be prepared to think and act both as specialists and as generalists in an increasingly complex world.

Rowan Gibson is founder and chairman of the Rethinking Group. Recently, he edited a series of essays written by some of the most respected leadership experts in the world for a book titled *Rethinking the Future*. After reviewing what these guiding lights had to say, Gibson firmly concluded that "the future will not be a continuation of the past. It will be a series of discontinuities." He called for an intellectual leap because, he said, "linear thinking is useless in a nonlinear world." Gibson described 21st century leaders as "those who stay ahead of the change curve, constantly redefining their industries, creating new markets, blazing new trails, reinventing the competitive rules, and challenging the status quo." He pleaded for "imagination." In summary, he remarked, "The road stops here ... the future will be different from the past; and new times call for new organizations." In deciding "where ... we go next," he stated, "we are going to need a vision, a destination, a point of view about the future" (2002, pp. 4–7, 10–11).

Leaders Capable of Creating a Future

Effective leaders. We often know them when we see them, but what sets them apart? What do they have in common?

Thoughtful observers suggest leaders share a number of distinct qualities. They are clarifiers, definers, critics, optimists, teachers, mobilizers, implementers, managers, and nurturers. They enjoy learning and thinking and aren't threatened by the unfamiliar. They may be forceful but are low key enough that people feel free to offer suggestions or question their ideas. They are collegial, with excellent people skills. They actually enjoy complexity and are not overwhelmed by constant change or by considering what that change might mean for what they do (Cleveland, 2002a). They also understand that the best in any profession is first a teacher.

What additional qualities should we expect from leaders in education (and other professions) who are capable of constantly shaping a future? Here are three:

- **Inclusiveness.** Effective leaders are inclusive. In education, leadership is not solely confined to the superintendent's or the principal's office. Because education is so critical to developing and realizing our hopes for the future, all educators, whatever positions they hold, should be considered and expected to be leaders by virtue of the key roles they play in society.
- **Connectedness.** Education leaders who will help shape our future may have specialized knowledge and skills, but they are able to see things in context. In short, they are eager to understand societal forces that will affect the whole of society, including their education system and their individual students. Harlan Cleveland, noted scholar, statesman, and futurist, refers to leadership as "the get-it-all-together profession" (2002b, p. 42).

- **Enthusiasm about the future.** Effective leaders in education are enthusiastic about preparing their schools and their students for the future. They spend little time defending the status quo. After all, the job of a leader is to define, not just defend.

Thomas Paine, prolific journalist of the Revolutionary War era, used his pen to garner support for forming a new nation on the North American continent. In his famed *Common Sense*, he clearly demonstrated his understanding of the impact of contemporary actions on the short- and long-term future. In "Thoughts on the Present State of American Affairs," Paine (1776) wrote, "'Tis not the affair of a city, a country, a province, or a kingdom.... 'Tis not the concern of a day, a year, or an age; posterity are virtually involved in this contest, and will be more or less affected, even to the end of time, by the proceedings now."

A present-day author, Alan Axelrod, offers another perspective on the relationship between the present and the future. In his book *Elizabeth I, CEO: Strategic Lessons from the Leader Who Built an Empire*, he says:

> The present is. The future, in contrast, only seems to be. It has no existence. Wishing for the best in the future is futile, useless, without effect. If we wish for the best, we must act on the present, which is all there is. Fortunately acting on the present does not rule out improving the future. Indeed, it is only by acting on the present reality that we can shape a future." (2000, p. 240)

This understanding of the relationship between the present and the future is part of what distinguishes *leaders* from *managers*. In *Learning to Lead: A Workbook on Becoming a Leader*, Warren Bennis, the distinguished professor of business administration at the University of Southern California, and Joan Goldsmith, a leading organizational consultant, created a chart showing the distinctions between managers and leaders (see Figure 1.1).

Important times cry for future-oriented thinkers. We are living during one of those times.

1.1	Distinctions Between a Manager and a Leader

- The manager **administers**; the leader **innovates**.
- The manager is a **copy**; the leader is **the original**.
- The manager **maintains**; the leader **develops**.
- The manager **accepts** reality; the leader **investigates** it.
- The manager focuses on **systems and structure**; the leader focuses on **people**.
- The manager relies on **control**; the leader inspires **trust**.
- The manager has a **short-range view**; the leader has a **long-range perspective**.
- The manager asks **how and when**; the leader asks **what and why**.
- The manager has her eye always on the **bottom line**; the leader has her eye on the **future**.
- The manager **imitates**; the leader **originates**.
- The manager **accepts the status quo**; the leader **challenges it**.
- The manager is the **classic good soldier**; the leader is her **own person**.
- **The manager does things right; the leader does the right things.**

Source: From *Learning to Lead*, 3rd ed. (pp. 8–9), by Warren Bennis and Joan Goldsmith, 2003, New York: Basic Books. Copyright 2003 by Basic Books.

The Struggle Between Depth and Breadth

"He's a mile wide but only half an inch deep." For decades, perhaps even centuries, that epithet has been thrown at people who know a little bit about a lot of things but aren't really specialists in anything. On the other hand, the description "jack of all trades, master of none" falls somewhere between an accolade and a stinging rebuke.

As the world accelerates and as new knowledge and events cascade into our lives, concern is growing about the leader who has plenty of depth but little or no breadth. The term *narrowness* describes the person who is, to turn the phrase, a mile deep and only half an inch wide.

Leadership experts trying to reshape organizations for a fast-changing world complain of what they call "stovepipes" or "silos." Some talk about the organization as a set of well-oiled gears, all turning but never connecting. For an organization to be effective, everyone on the team needs to be connected—to share a broad understanding of overall purpose. The sense of urgency for making those connections has increased. At one time we said that working together would increase our effectiveness. More recently we've added another stark reality—working together is the *only* way to improve our chances of survival as an education system, as a community, as a nation, and as a world.

The charge of narrowness is leveled at people in virtually thousands of industries and professions. Even educators take the rap. "After all," some people ask, "how can educators prepare students for an increasingly complex world if they don't have broad knowledge, broad interests, and broad experiences themselves?"

Context is crucial. Everything we do affects everything else. Press an inflated balloon here, and it bulges out there. The program that guarantees unprecedented benefits for some might bring devastating side effects for others.

Narrowness is often built into the system. In business, education, or government, one department or discipline might be forced to fight the others for scarce resources. In medicine, the ear, nose, and throat specialist, an otorhinolaryngologist, might tell you that the infection has moved to your chest. Therefore, you'll need to see a pulmonologist. Meanwhile, the general practitioner, overwhelmed with treating colds, flu, and a host of other maladies, refers patients to specialists. There are many parallels in education.

The question becomes, who is, or who should be, looking out for the total system, whether it's an individual human being or some other species, a business, a school or college, an industry or profession, or maybe even the planet itself?

The answer is, the person who is capable of being an intellectually curious, thoughtful, experienced, and connected generalist.

Specializing Without Isolating

Members of the distinguished advisory council for this book offered comments about the tug-of-war between the roles of specialist and generalist. Here are a few of those comments.

"In addition to being a generalist, the leader must have some area of thorough content expertise in order to have … credibility within the area that he or she is leading," says Drew Albritten, executive director of the Council for Exceptional Children. "The generalist half can be a visionary, just as the specialist half is fiscally and legally responsible," he adds.

"I think it is true that leaders must be generalists, but I do not think they can only be that," says Douglas Greenberg, president and CEO of the Shoah Foundation. "They must also have some area of special knowledge and expertise that confers legitimacy, something that distinguishes them as especially experienced, knowledgeable, and competent in some area of the organization's interests." Greenberg concludes, "You should know something, anything, deeply to be a good leader, and you need to be smart enough to learn almost anything else."

Carol G. Peck, the 1991 National Superintendent of the Year and now president and CEO of the Rodel Charitable Foundation, notes, "It is true that a good leader must be a generalist, but that alone is not enough. On many occasions, it is essential that the leader use specific experience and knowledge to deliver credible solutions to complex problems."

"Increasingly, specialist expertise will be benchmarked against world-class standards and best practices worldwide," suggests Frank Method, an international relations professional who is currently director of education policy for the Research Triangle Institute (RTI), International. He also believes that learning objectives will include "preparation for participation in the global economy, with an expectation that many, perhaps most, students will be employed by firms and organizations working internationally, trading internationally, or providing services internationally." Some, Method predicts, may actually "reside locally but travel and work outside the United States."

Michael Silver, a veteran education leader who currently serves as director and assistant professor of education administration at Seattle University, remarks, "A leader with significant decision-making responsibilities must be able to integrate perspectives across the entire organization. In dealing with the complexities of today's organizations, the leader as generalist has a better vantage point to view the organization. The leader can gather information by continually scanning the internal organization and the world outside for trends, patterns, and factors to make the connections and shape the direction for the organization's success. In short, the leader as generalist can achieve results while searching for, and maintaining, an openness to new ideas, regardless of where in the world they arise."

Learning Across Disciplines

Education has many roles. It helps develop people's knowledge, skills, and behaviors. It enlightens and brings out the genius that is already there. In the process, educators hope to shape good citizens who are employable and capable of living interesting, fulfilling, productive, and ethical lives.

Increasingly, the employable, interested, and cultivated citizen is expected to find relationships across bodies of knowledge, ideas, and cultures. Of course, that means educators at all levels, while pursuing their specialties, will also need to have broad interests. Those curiosities will help them orchestrate learning across disciplines.

At its best, the very process of cross-disciplinary education reveals the chaotic white spaces separating disparate ideas and helps students discover relationships among those ideas. The process of connecting ideas in turn stokes the fire of knowledge creation and breakthrough thinking and serves as a powerful engine for the advancement of our economy and civil society.

Considering the vast array of talents, interests, abilities, and intelligences that students bring to the classroom, this noble effort will depend on people who are not only specialists but also connected generalists.

More and more, educators will be expected to have broad interests and a constantly developing range of knowledge and skills.

In a bold statement, Harvard biologist and sage Edward O. Wilson (1998) ventures, "The ongoing fragmentation of knowledge and resulting chaos in philosophy are not reflections of the real world but artifacts of scholarship" (p. 8). Revealing his feistiness and commitment to bringing some unity to knowledge, Wilson remarks that the enlightened person is "ignorant of nothing" and that "nothing is beneath his attention" (p. 18).

A Curriculum for Life

At the turn of the 21st century, I, along with Harvey Long and Frank With-row, directed a project that brought together a noted council of 21 leaders in business, education, government, and other fields. We provided advice for a study that resulted in a book published by the American Association of School Administrators, titled *Preparing Schools and School Systems for the 21st Century* (Withrow, 1999). The council offered the following sage advice: Schools will need to offer "a project-based curriculum for life that engages students in addressing real-world problems, issues important to humanity, and questions that matter." To be prepared for life in a global knowledge/ information age, the study declared, students "need to be prepared in liberal studies, including but not limited to math, science, literature, the arts, culture, history, civics, philosophy, and communication skills." They will need to "be prepared for responsible citizenship in a democracy . . . develop characteristics of goodness and learn to treat other people well." Participation in the arts, the study reported, "should help students develop their creative talents, and our approach to education should encourage students to think outside the box" (p. 9).

The Journey Begins

In Chapter 2 we begin the journey to effective leadership by exploring 12 principles that could serve as a guide for connected, future-oriented leaders. Consider how we might apply these principles in the education system or in any other organization. How should they guide us as leaders? Do they have implications for us as we think about how to help students become leaders in the future?

Questions and Activities

1. List 20 reasons why educators need to be connected with the broader environment.
2. Consider Bennis and Goldsmith's distinctions between a manager and leader. What distinctions would you add?
3. What was Gandhi getting at when he said, "Look below the surface and identify the hidden and unarticulated needs that others cannot see, and create a bond with those you are trying to serve"?
4. What do leaders capable of creating a future have in common?

Readings

Bennis, W., & Goldsmith, J. (2003). *Learning to lead: A workbook on becoming a leader* (3rd ed.). New York: Basic Books.

Cleveland, H. (2002). *Nobody in charge: Essays on the future of leadership*. San Francisco: Jossey-Bass.

Gibson, R. (Ed.). (2002). *Rethinking the future*. Sonoma, CA: Nicholas Brealey Publishing.

Surowiecki, J. (2004). *The wisdom of crowds*. New York: Doubleday.

2 | Guiding Principles for Future-Oriented Leaders

If your actions inspire others to dream more, learn more, do more, and become more, you are a leader.

—John Quincy Adams

How can we become enlightened and connected leaders who are capable of creating a future? What do we need to think about, and what do we need to do? This chapter presents a number of principles that reinforce the point that no institution should be isolated. To be truly effective, educators need to be connected to an array of people and ideas, and must in turn help connect their students with the world outside the classroom.

The 12 Principles

Figure 2.1 lists 12 guiding principles for connected, future-oriented leaders. We explore each principle in the sections that follow. Keep in mind that the list of thoughts, beliefs, and behaviors is far from exhaustive. Its purpose is to stimulate further thinking. What would you add to the list?

Curiosity, persistence, imagination, and genuine interest are the main power sources for futures thinking. People who are curious and persistent are people who will be educated for the rest of their lives. Of course, the downside of being curious is having an interest in nearly everything. It's hard to turn off the curiosity. The upside is that people who are curious generally live much more interesting lives. They are constantly finding

2.1	Guiding Principles for Connected, Future-Oriented Leaders

1. Curiosity, persistence, imagination, and genuine interest are the main power sources for futures thinking.
2. Breadth and depth are both important.
3. Leaders connect the dots and seek common ground.
4. There are more than two sides to most issues.
5. The future is not necessarily a straight-line projection of the present.
6. Enlightenment and isolation are becoming opposites.
7. Peripheral vision can help us avoid being blindsided.
8. A belief in synergy can spark knowledge creation and breakthrough thinking.
9. Collateral opportunity and collateral damage both deserve our attention.
10. Bringing out the best in others is basic.
11. Courage and personal responsibility need to overcome fear and self-pity.
12. The role of strategic futurist is part of everybody's job.

relationships between people and ideas. Connected leaders are noted for their curiosity, persistence, and genuine interests that extend far beyond their immediate job or profession.

Breadth and depth are both important. Some things are best taught through precept and example. In this case, the precept is that both breadth and depth are important. What follows is a real-life example.

When the East Building of the National Gallery of Art in Washington, D.C., was under construction, the project involved one of the longest continuous pours of concrete in history. A few days before the wet mortar started rolling in, construction workers with a broad array of specialties were invited to a meeting. In addition to hearing about logistics, these hard hats were shown a model of the completed building. One of the workers is reported to have said, "If we don't do a good job vibrating that concrete, people will see it for a thousand years." Welders, carpenters, masons, managers, and a host of others were no longer just "doing their individual jobs" or practicing their specialized skills. People of great skill and significant depth discovered, as one, the breadth of their responsibility. They were united in building one of the world's leading art galleries and their own personal legacy.

Leaders connect the dots and seek common ground. Ideas and information converge. Nearly everything is interconnected. A crop failure in Ukraine can directly affect the price of a loaf of bread in the United States. The inability to read can depress achievement in math because students may not be able to comprehend story problems. A lack of cultural understanding can lead to crisis and conflict that eventually diverts resources that might have been used to feed the hungry, support medical research, and generally improve the standard of living.

No matter how big or small the threat, the opportunity, or the simple need, the connected leader takes responsibility for pulling together the ideas and the people who can deal with it. True leaders are also able to back off, to stand at the edges of a conflict, and to articulate what we have in common—our common ground—and then unite us in common purpose. During the height of the Cold War, nations on both sides of the political and economic divide came together to develop a network of weather satellites. Reminders of the threat of nuclear holocaust have persuaded countries in conflict to step back from the brink. Environmental concerns such as global warming have brought disparate groups together in common purpose.

There are more than two sides to most issues. Concern has grown that people, countries, regions, and the world itself are becoming increasingly polarized. More and more we hear people telling us that our choices are either black or white, with no shades of gray: "It's my way or the highway." Most of us can recall the voice of a parent, a friend, or a politician reminding us that "there are two sides to every issue."

Attuned to a multitude of opinions and a constant flow of ideas and information, the thoughtful, connected leader knows there may be several sides to an issue, not just two. All deserve consideration in moving toward consensus or in making a decision.

Data-driven decisions have become a basic part of most organizations. Some might put it this way: "You either employ data-driven decision making or you don't." In education, some might ask, "What data are you using to make your decisions? Are you using only test data, or do you use demographic data that point out changes in your community? Do you consider the emergence of new careers and the demand for people who can be effective citizens in a democratic society? Do you consider things that are important for the educated person to know and be able to do that can't readily be tested?"

Black and white and either/or aren't what they used to be.

The future is not necessarily a straight-line projection of the present. John C. Calhoun, a member of the U.S. Congress and vice president during the early 1800s, is said to have advised, "Invest in canals; the railroads will never amount to anything." Surely others of his time were busy developing better buggy whips.

Little did they know that by the end of their century the first automobile would take to the roads—at the time a confused network of buggy trails. How could they have known that the Wright brothers would demonstrate powered flight in 1903? How could they have known that Samuel Langley and Robert Goddard would conduct experiments in aeronautics and rocketry that eventually took us into space and made air transportation a primary means of getting around?

As generalists, as specialists, and as connected leaders, we need to constantly be involved in the business of creating a future. As educators, we need to be sure our students are engaged in futures activities and futures studies, and that they are capable of articulating and pursuing the philosophy of possibility.

Those who blithely say, "This is how it is, and this is how it's going to be" probably need to pay more attention to scientific developments, world events, and the cadence of history. Breakthroughs depend on each of us. We can only coast downhill.

Enlightenment and isolation are becoming opposites. Quiet moments are valuable in helping us find perspective. Reflection is essential. Self-discovery and spiritual renewal can help give greater meaning to our lives. In fact, a legitimate trend toward introspection is developing in reaction to an environment that has us connected at a frantic 24/7. However, thoughtfulness is not tantamount to withdrawal or escape from the needs of others. That type of self-centeredness is sometimes called selfishness. Even writer Henry David Thoreau, known for his retreats into nature, is cited as a citizen who demanded improvements in social institutions. He both reached in and reached out.

Today, much of the world's information is readily available at the click of a mouse. Satellite communication, high-speed computers, and frequent travel have opened a window on much of what happens on the planet. Whether we choose to pay attention is up to us.

The double-edged nature of many technologies has raised concerns. Although access to information can motivate our actions, it can also take on a life of its own. It's not enough to become isolated, glued to the computer screen or the hundreds of channels readily available by satellite or broadband. We need to consider how we will act based on what we've learned.

Yesterday, people were often "well informed" or "uninformed." Today the scale has broadened. Now there is a good chance that we'll be seen as either "enlightened" or "isolated."

Peripheral vision can help us avoid being blindsided. How often have we heard this comment: "I just didn't see it coming"? The connected leader not only sees straight ahead but also uses peripheral vision. Visionary leaders are constantly looking for ideas and trends outside their immediate field that could affect their hopes, dreams, possibilities, research, plans, and markets. Enlightened leaders also pay particular attention to how what they have on the drawing board might affect others.

Pearl Harbor, 9/11, the effect of contraception on birth rates—we didn't see them coming. The effect of cell phones on how we communicate—we didn't see it coming. With improved peripheral vision, we might have been better prepared. A more comfortable explanation is that these things just happened "out of the blue."

A belief in synergy can spark knowledge creation and breakthrough thinking. Harlan Cleveland (2002a) calls leaders the "get-it-all-together" people. The generalist role, he says, is "about integrative thinking, about making what hasn't happened before happen now." Leaders are "the glue that holds people together and the imagination around which other people mobilize." Their concern for "the general outcome," rather than simply promoting their specific interests, stimulates thinking (p. 13).

The informed, experienced generalist knows that the search for relationships can create synergy. That synergy, stimulated by communication and working across disciplines, can lead to breakthrough thinking and the creation of new knowledge. In turn, that new knowledge can lead to new products, revolutionary techniques for educating children, or fresh ideas for breaking an impasse among nations or groups that might be in conflict.

Collateral opportunity and collateral damage both deserve our attention. When we think and work across disciplines, we see things in a new light. In some cases, opportunities are hidden from us because we are simply too insular to see them.

By broadening our vision, we are better able to see both the positive and the potentially devastating effects of our plans. With these insights, we can pursue "collateral opportunities" while avoiding what has become known in military circles as "collateral damage."

Consider the example of education reform in the United States. The demand for reform was present. Educators had an opportunity to seize the initiative, to convene the nation in a substantive effort to create schools of the future. However, some other leaders in society thought the education system was committed to defending the status quo. When noneducators took the lead, often doing an end run around what they considered "the education establishment," they sometimes imposed programs and requirements that educators didn't necessarily like.

Connected leaders understand the importance of convening the meetings, listening to divergent points of view, coalescing the energy and ideas of a broad list of constituents, and generally taking the initiative.

Bringing out the best in others is basic. The effective generalist is a talent scout. Although some people in leadership positions spend a good deal of time with their own kind "because they're the only ones who really understand the depth of my responsibility," others are listening to people with different backgrounds and experiences. Across departmental, organizational, and national boundaries, these leaders find excitement in discovering the talents of other people, learning from their experiences, and hearing their concerns. Often they become mentors with a host of protégés. They play to people's strengths. They are masters at forming teams and bringing people together who can develop an idea or deal with a challenge. When confronted with a problem, these connected leaders are likely to say, "Let me suggest some people who might be helpful to you. They're all interested in this issue, and they have a huge variety of experience."

Courage and personal responsibility need to overcome fear and self-pity. "A little knowledge is a dangerous thing." "Let sleeping dogs lie." "What we don't know can't hurt us." The avoidance of personal responsibility drives a plethora of clichés, all of which carry a grain of truth.

Consider, for example, the pursuit of equal opportunity and justice. Martin Luther King Jr. was a motivated generalist who also had a focused purpose. He rallied people from many walks of life and made clear the connection between opportunity and justice for all and the very future of his country and the world. King said, "The ultimate measure of a man is not where he stands in moments of comfort and convenience, but where he stands at times of challenge and controversy."

Every leader who is fully aware of and sensitive to the needs of others is confronted with inequities and injustices. First reactions might include "Why me?" or "I was happier not knowing." Competition for resources to deal with problems or meet needs may be intense. Those in the majority who have advantages may not consider providing opportunities for the disadvantaged as a priority. However, people in communities nationwide and worldwide depend on the generalist who can see the need, who can articulate it clearly, who can spot possible unintended consequences, and who has the courage to lead the charge.

The role of strategic futurist is part of everybody's job. Futurists and forecasters generally try to be deep generalists. They attempt to stay in touch with what has happened in the past, what is happening now, and what might happen in the future. They also help us think about political, economic, social, technological, environmental, and other issues as we chart our courses. They spot and follow trends and encourage us to think deeply about the implications of those trends, and they're constantly urging people and organizations to consider what they want to become.

Futures thinking is not just for futurists. It's for everyone. The need to think in terms of the future is especially important for educators, whose prime commitment is preparing students for tomorrow's realities.

Other Perspectives on Leadership

Leadership in the new millennium will require great flexibility, courage, and integrity, Nobel Peace Prize recipients told attendees at a 2001 conference of the Greater Washington Society of Association Executives (GWSAE). Lech Walesa, the Polish activist and president whose Solidarity movement gave momentum to a social revolution in Poland and ended communism in that country, put it this way: "This new era requires new frameworks for institutions, both political and economic. Leaders must be more active and get others involved." Oscar Arias, former president of Costa Rica who negotiated a peace plan for nine Latin American countries, declared that "the qualities leaders need are character, a bold temperament, and, if possible, knowledge and intelligence." He advised, "Tell people what they want to know, not [just] what they want to hear." Arias also called for "an international code of conduct. Leadership should not put profits before principles" (Merriman-Clarke, 2001).

At an annual conference of the World Future Society, Bradley Hoyt (2003), a partner at Williams Inference Services in Mainville, Ohio, described the changing nature of organizations and how that change affects leadership. "Since the beginning of time, there have been two structures operating in every organization: hierarchy and networks," he said. "The hierarchy has been the focus, but today, networks are becoming more and more important."

Hoyt predicts a change from "economies of scale to economies of scope," with value moving "from physical products to knowledge products." Scale assumes that the bigger the factory, the more efficient it will be. Scope, on the other hand, operates on the premise that building knowledge and collaboration inside and outside the organization is what will really get the job done.

With value creation slipping from goods to services, Hoyt sees the decline of "dependent physical organizations" and the rise of "interdependent knowledge organizations." To make his point, he describes the organization of Detroit's auto industry as traditionally large and fixed, while pointing out that Hollywood's film industry and the high-tech firms of Silicon Valley tend to be generally small and fluid. Rather than assuming that a fixed group of people can do everything, a Hollywood producer pulls together the most knowledgeable, experienced people who can get the job done within a certain time frame for a fixed amount of money. The producer is a generalist who knows the capabilities, talents, interests, and experiences of a vast array of people. A team is selected that often connects directors, cinematographers, sound and lighting experts, actors, set designers, location scouts, wardrobe designers, public relations professionals, set photographers, advertising agency staff, accountants, and sometimes even educators, historians, and futurists. This group works together with a high level of intensity to meet myriad production challenges as they create a product, generally a feature film or a commercial.

Education is clearly in the business of offering one of the most valuable services in any society. To be effective, schools and colleges need to be interdependent knowledge organizations.

Questions and Activities

1. Review the 12 guiding principles for connected, future-oriented leaders discussed in this chapter. Add four more principles you believe should have been included.
2. Ask students to review the 12 guiding principles. Then ask them to identify six qualities they would like to see in a person who might someday be their supervisor, or in a person who might get their vote as president of their country.

Readings

Cleveland, H. (2002). *Nobody in charge: Essays on the future of leadership.* San Francisco: Jossey-Bass.

PART 2

Tools and Techniques for Scanning the Environment

Future-focused leaders face what seems like a daunting task. They are expected to be constantly in touch with the environment—with trends, issues, and other forces that affect their organization, industry, or profession. Any one of those trends, issues, or forces will likely enhance or inhibit their progress or ultimate success.

Part 2 explores tools and techniques for reading the internal and external environment, from identifying and analyzing trends and issues to discovering gaps between where we are now and where we would like to be in the future.

3 | The Importance of Being Connected—Internally and Externally

*Every step we take—no matter how small—
to understand the needs of other people we
strive to serve will increase our bond with
them and move us in the direction of a higher
standard of leadership.*

—Keshevan Nair (1994)

Leaders are generally good at stepping forward to solve problems and pursue opportunities. It goes with the territory. However, stepping forward is not enough. Frequently, maybe even as a habit, we also need to step back, to take a longer view of the internal and external environment.

What do we mean by "environment"? *Webster's New Collegiate Dictionary* (2004) defines it as "the aggregate of social and cultural conditions that influence the life of an individual or community" (p. 418).

What are the benefits of using effective processes for staying close to the environment? Certainly the tools and techniques we use to get organized and stay in touch can give us from a few to several thousand "ears to the ground." They can also enhance our foresight.

According to the World Future Society (WFS), "Foresight gives us increased power to shape our futures, even in the most turbulent of times." In the May–June 2004 issue of *The Futurist* magazine, WFS points out, "We often think people are successful because they are just lucky, when in fact it was their foresight that made them 'lucky.' It enabled them to take advantage of opportunities and to avoid problems that trap other people" (p. 32).

How can we gain that foresight? Perspective and context are critical in positioning any organization or individual for the future—in gaining foresight. To hone our perspective and understand the context that surrounds us, we need to regularly scan the environment.

Scanning the Environment

Why is scanning important? Here are a few basic reasons. First, scanning can help us identify opportunities. As we scan the environment, we can get a lead on emerging developments, spot trends, and make connections with ideas from many sources. Scanning has a tendency to stimulate thinking and tap ingenuity. In fact, the very process can help build multiple connections and relationships with organizations and people who may be crucial to our ultimate success, whether we realize it or not.

Second, scanning can help us avoid walking, or even running at full speed, into a swamp filled with alligators. Although surprises are exhilarating, most of us would prefer to avoid those devastating, unexpected ones if at all possible. If we need to take risks, demonstrate an extra amount of courage, or take on an uphill battle, we should do it with our eyes wide open. Clem Bezold, president of the Institute for Alternative Futures (IAF), puts it best when he reminds us that "scanning can improve our peripheral vision" (Bezold, Rhea, & Rowley, 2003).

What individuals and groups should be included in our scan? In answering that question, we need to look both internally and externally. Certainly we'll want to understand the thinking of people inside the organization. However, it's also imperative that we get a bead on what's happening in our industry or profession and consider broad and profound political, economic, social, technological, and other forces affecting the whole of society.

By expanding the scope of our environmental scanning, we bring others inside our tent. As a result, we end up with information and ideas that are critical to us in shaping a future, and we also expand our community of interest. When we consider societal forces, we're in a better position to make our organization more viable and better able to serve its clients. We're also more effectively poised to raise issues, set trends, get the resources we need, and generally become a more effective force in our own right.

By systematically listening, both internally and externally, we build relationships and glean information. These then serve as building blocks of our social and intellectual capital. Who we know and what we know both count.

Systematic listening with the intent of getting a handle on an ever-changing environment may seem like a daunting task. Where do we begin? Let's start by thinking about what we might need to know from our external and internal communities.

An External Scan

If we hope to have a sound vision, viable goals, and relevant objectives for our organization, then we'd better be connected to the community we serve. Surely, as we define "community," we will need to consider families, neighborhoods, towns, and cities. However, information and transportation technologies have virtually shrunk the globe, so we are literally forced to think of ourselves as members of our national and world communities. Myopia is out. The broad view is in.

An external scan will likely include the following activities:

- Identifying social, political, economic, technological, environmental, and other trends
- Reviewing opportunities and threats
- Seeking and considering the views of leading thinkers
- Considering other emerging developments and when their impact might become commonplace
- Collecting and studying demographics of a total community or even targeted constituencies

- Gathering information about psychographics—people's views and attitudes—to get a clearer view of what people value and what motivates them.

An Internal Scan

Organizations that create synergy, that stand out because of their uncanny ability to become greater than the sum of their parts, are constantly listening and learning. "We need to change the way we think about learning and interacting with each other at all levels," suggests leadership expert Peter Senge (2002, p. 129). Without these ongoing connections, we shortchange our intellectual capacity and our ability to collaboratively solve problems or pursue opportunities.

Board, staff, consultants—in fact, anyone who serves an organization—are all part of its brain trust. Some might play highly specialized roles. When we regularly engage specialists in both internal and external environmental scans, we not only enrich the organization with their unique insights, but also help them become even more connected generalists.

An internal scan might include the following activities:

- Reviewing the history of the organization and the industry
- Defining the culture
- Considering stakeholders
- Looking at financial health
- Speculating on possible competition
- Reviewing actual programs and performance in comparison with the stated vision or specific targets (e.g., tracing student achievement and what might be influencing it)
- Gathering and considering data that reflect continuous improvement in products and services and in the processes that make them possible
- Considering the organization's reputation

- Identifying possible strengths and weaknesses
- Auditing how the organization does or does not communicate
- Discussing root causes and defining moments to help understand the origins of problems, successes, and opportunities
- Speculating on the organization's or industry's flexibility for change

Universal Techniques for Reading the Environment

Before we consider the specific tools and techniques for scanning the environment that are discussed in the next several chapters, let's explore a few of the most universal methods people and organizations use to read the environment, to listen, and to generate ideas. Each can be used in nearly any type of environmental scan, and each could be the subject for separate books. These methods are polling and interviews, focus groups, and brainstorming.

Polling and Interviews: Getting a Snapshot of Ideas and Opinions

Obviously, there are many ways of getting counsel from others. Some of that consultation takes place one-on-one or in small- or large-group meetings. Extending the reach of that counsel often involves formal or informal polls. Well-conceived questionnaires (distributed by regular mail or e-mail) and interviews (conducted in person, by phone, or online) can provide quick and helpful snapshots of ideas or opinions.

Because entire books have been devoted to polling, here we are only acknowledging how beneficial it can be, confident that future-oriented leaders already have some understanding of the process and its importance or have access to people who do.

Focus Groups: Enriching Decisions with Qualitative Research

What's more common than the scoreboard mentality? People seem to want education scores the same way they get baseball, football, basketball, hockey, or soccer scores. Educators feel repeated frustration as reading, math, or other test scores are headlined in a newspaper or flashed on a television screen. "They're comparing oranges and apples." "The tests don't measure what we're teaching." "They're ignoring the degree of difficulty we face." Comments such as these reflect just the tip of the frustration iceberg as people make judgments based on limited poll or test results, on data that do not provide subtle and essential information.

Quantitative research crackles throughout society, and it is often shaped to fit the needs of partisan politics. "Are you *for* welfare reform or *against* it?" The pat answers reflected in the results may be dramatic, but they don't help explain the many shades of gray between "for" and "against." That's just one of many reasons people and organizations are adding qualitative research to their mix of environmental scanning tools and why focus groups have grown in popularity and prominence.

Focus groups can help us move from the general to the specific. They can provide a way to test new ideas. They can give us fairly direct hints of how people feel about an existing product or service and how it might be improved. These groups can also help us get a better understanding of the environment as we go through the process of constructing formal or informal opinion polls or move forward with various other scanning tools.

What are focus groups? Some people describe them as interviews, but with more than one person. In fact, the interview might be conducted with 6 to 10 people, all at the same time. What are the steps involved in putting together focus groups? Here are six, adapted from a longer list developed by Carter McNamara (2005):

1. **Set an objective.** Define the major objective of your meeting.

2. **Develop questions.** Develop five or six questions that you want the group to explore. As you compose the questions, consider the problem or need that should be addressed.

3. **Plan a meeting.** Schedule the focus group meeting, allowing up to 90 minutes for the discussion.

4. **Set ground rules.** Be clear about ground rules for the meeting. Those rules might include the need to focus on the question at hand, to be sure every person is engaged, to maintain momentum by not getting bogged down in supporting or refuting one person's opinion, and to make everyone in the group feel comfortable with participating, no matter how divergent their views.

5. **Record ideas and information.** Carefully record each person's response, on paper and perhaps even on video or audiotape. Allow a minute or two at the conclusion of each segment to summarize the ideas and opinions expressed in response to a question.

6. **Put what you've learned to work.** Use what you've learned to inform your organization's thinking, possibly your decisions, and maybe the construction of a more scientifically administered questionnaire.

Brainstorming: Releasing Ingenuity and Productive Thinking

We all know how some meetings go. We get together to come up with ideas. One person makes a suggestion, and we discuss it until the meeting adjourns.

If we truly hope to release ingenuity and encourage productive thinking, then we need to use brainstorming techniques. Brainstorming is a key tool that applies to most problem-solving and future-oriented meetings. In fact, brainstorming techniques are an assumed component in many of the environmental scanning processes discussed in this chapter. Here are some basic rules of the road for brainstorming:

- **Encourage free expression of ideas.** A facilitator of the meeting should explain that everyone's ideas will be heard and recorded. One thing to make clear is that the only bad idea is the one that isn't expressed. The goal is productive thinking.
- **Encourage everyone's participation.** Be sure everyone who is involved, or as many as possible, actually participates in the process. Write down every idea in a way that can be readily understood.
- **Avoid killer phrases that close down communication.** Killer phrases are comments such as these: "What a silly idea!" "I wouldn't do that in a million years." "You've really lost it on that one."
- **Sort the results.** When the brainstorming portion of the meeting or program is completed, you may want to have the group sort the suggestions by considering their probability, impact, implications, and priorities. This step is optional.

The Importance of Environmental Scanning

Information and ideas—and the processes we use to get them—are critical. Environmental scanning helps us gather information and ideas. If done well and in the proper spirit, the scanning processes can generate excitement and produce a cascade of valuable thinking. Rather than producing fear about change, involvement in the scanning process can increase *esprit de corps* and open our eyes to real and possible opportunities, cautions, and problems that need our attention.

Environmental scanning also helps us understand the larger context in which data reside. Data-driven decisions are important—no doubt about it. However, using data to arbitrarily set direction without understanding the broader environment in which we operate can lead to disaster. The various tools and techniques described in this and the following chapters are intended to take us a step beyond what most of us would consider basic, such as data on student achievement and organizational performance, demographic information, ongoing reviews of literature, database and Web site searches, and scholarly research. Attention to these sources of information should be both serious and ongoing, but rather than considering such information in isolation, we can enhance its value by connecting it to the larger world in which we live and work through environmental scanning.

Questions and Activities

1. List five reasons why scanning the internal and external environment is important as we attempt to shape an organization for the future.
2. Form a focus group to glean thinking on a topic of your choice following the guidelines included in this chapter. After the focus group meeting, ask, "How could we have improved the process?"
3. Select a problem that needs to be solved or an issue that you feel should be addressed. Lead a group in brainstorming how to deal with it, applying the four basic rules found in this chapter. Again, when the process is completed, ask, "How could we have improved the process?" Did everyone participate? Did the group engage in productive thinking or dwell on just a few items? Did people in the group use any "killer phrases"?

Readings

Nair, K. (1994). *A higher standard of leadership: Lessons from the life of Gandhi*. Emeryville, CA: Berrett-Koehler.

Senge, P. (2004). Rethinking control and complexity. In R. Gibson (Ed.), *Rethinking the future* (pp. 122–146). London: Nicholas Brealey Publishing.

4 Trends: Identifying and Analyzing Their Impact

There's a battle outside, and it's a-ragin'. It'll soon shake your windows and rattle your walls, for the times they are a-changin'.

—Bob Dylan (1964)

Whatever happened to the status quo? Did it ever exist, or was it a figment of our imaginations? Has there ever been a time when we could freeze the world and preserve it just as it was? The title of a popular Broadway musical of the 1960s captures a feeling many of us share at times: *Stop the World—I Want to Get Off.*

We take snapshots, fill museums, produce yearbooks, and write our own versions of history. Most of us are intent on capturing the moment. For many of us, in fact, savoring those moments is becoming increasingly important, because we know that they will eventually add up to decades, lifetimes, centuries, and millennia.

All of us hope for a brighter future. Together, we're navigating the third millennium, and we're destined to do it without that safe haven called the status quo. That's why knowing how to recognize and navigate trends and issues is fast becoming a basic skill.

Author's note: This chapter condenses information that appears in another book I have written, *16 Trends: Their Profound Impact on Our Future* (in press), published by the Educational Research Service (ERS) in Arlington, Virginia. *16 Trends* provides an in-depth exploration of social, economic, political, technological, environmental, demographic, and other forces and speculates on their possible implications for education.

In this chapter we identify and analyze trends that could have a significant effect on the social landscape. Some of these trends represent seismic shifts. They are shaking the very foundations of society as we've known it. Each will have profound implications for education. After all, our education systems—and other organizations, for that matter—are a part of society, not separate from it.

Trends and Tipping Points

Trends can lead to tipping points. If we are aware of trends and constantly considering their implications, then we are more likely ready to adjust as the world changes. As connected leaders, we might even be able to manage our response to these trends so that they actually tip our way.

What Are Trends?

Howard Chase (1984), the father of issue management, described trends as "detectable changes which precede issues" (p. 38). *Webster's New Collegiate Dictionary* (2004) defines a *trend* as "a line of general direction or movement; a prevailing tendency or inclination" (p. 1334).

Trends can help in *forecasting* possible futures. Mastering the art and science of dealing with trends can also help us in *backcasting*—determining the future we would like to see and then proactively generating the trends or activities that are most likely to get us there. One more thing: if we play our cards right, *trend setting* is a distinct possibility.

Implications for Education and Society

Figure 4.1 lists 16 political, economic, social, technological, demographic, environmental, and other trends that will profoundly impact education and the whole of society in the 21st century. As you review each of these trends, ask yourself or engage others in addressing key questions about their potential impact. For anyone concerned about education, two of those questions might be the following:

4.1	16 Trends That Will Profoundly Affect Education and the Whole of Society in the 21st Century

Note: The symbol → indicates a clear, nearly unmitigated trend from one condition to the next, while ↔ indicates a trend that can be expected to develop or continue based on evidence and the reality that certain existing conditions are very likely unsustainable. In some cases, a tug is evident between current and future conditions.

1. **For the first time in history, the old will outnumber the young.**
   (Younger → Older) (Worldwide: Developed World: Younger → Older, Underdeveloped World: Older → Younger)

2. **Majorities will become minorities, creating ongoing challenges for social cohesion.**
   (Majority/Minority → Minority/Majority)
   (Worldwide: Diversity = Division ↔ Diversity = Enrichment)

3. **Social and intellectual capital will become economic drivers, intensifying competition for well-educated people.**
   (Industrial Age → Global Knowledge/Information Age)

4. **Standards and high-stakes tests will fuel a demand for personalization in an education system increasingly committed to lifelong human development.**
   (Standardization → Personalization)

5. **The Millennial Generation will insist on solutions to accumulated problems and injustices, while an emerging Generation E will call for equilibrium.**
   (GIs, Silents, Boomers, Xers → Millennials, Generation E)

6. **Continuous improvement and collaboration will replace quick fixes and defense of the status quo.**
   (Quick Fixes/Status Quo → Continuous Improvement)

7. **Technology will increase the speed of communication and the pace of advancement or decline.**
   (Atoms → Bits) (Macro → Micro → Nano → Subatomic)

8. **Release of human ingenuity will become a primary responsibility of education and society.**
   (Information Acquisition → Knowledge Creation and Breakthrough Thinking)

4.1	16 Trends That Will Profoundly Affect Education and the Whole of Society in the 21st Century (cont.)

9. **Pressure will grow for society to prepare people for jobs and careers that may not currently exist.**
(Career Preparation ↔ Career Adaptability)

10. **Competition will increase to attract and keep qualified educators.**
(High Demand ↔ Even Higher Demand)

11. **Scientific discoveries and societal realities will force widespread ethical choices.**
(Pragmatic/Expedient → Ethical)

12. **Common opportunities and threats will intensify a worldwide demand for planetary security.**
(Personal Security/Self Interest ↔ Planetary Security)
(Common Threats ↔ Common Opportunities)

13. **Understanding will grow that sustained poverty is expensive, debilitating, and unsettling.**
(Sustained Poverty ↔ Opportunity and Hope)

14. **Polarization and narrowness will bend toward reasoned discussion, evidence, and consideration of varying points of view.**
(Narrowness ↔ Open-Mindedness)

15. **As nations vie for understanding and respect in an interdependent world, international learning, including diplomatic skills, will become basic. (Subtrend: To earn respect in an interdependent world, nations will be expected to demonstrate their reliability and tolerance.)**
(Isolationist Independence ↔ Interdependence)

16. **Greater numbers of people will seek personal meaning in their lives in response to an intense, high-tech, always-on, fast-moving society.**
(Personal Accomplishment ↔ Personal Meaning)

Source: From *16 Trends: Their Profound Impact on Our Future,* by Gary Marx and Educational Research Service, in press, Arlington, VA: Educational Research Service. Copyright 2005 by Gary Marx and Educational Research Service.

- What are the implications of these trends for how we operate our education system?
- What are the implications of these trends for what our students need to know and be able to do—their academic knowledge, their skills, their behaviors, and their attitudes?

Spotting and Analyzing Trends

Every future-focused leader constantly has an ear to the ground. Spotting trends is a never-ending responsibility, but it's an exciting one. Being aware of possible trends is one of the first and most essential steps on the road to creating an even brighter future.

In some cases, as future-focused leaders we might spot trends through intuition. Things just seem to start adding up. We might see or hear similar ideas or concerns popping up in our reading, listening, or conversations. We might be among the millions of people who visit Web sites such as those operated by the U.S. Census Bureau (http://www.census.gov) and the U.S. Bureau of Labor Statistics (http://www.bls.gov) for information on such things as the growth and makeup of the U.S. population, fast-growing careers, and employment/unemployment reports. Or we might be among those who do formal content analysis, systematically counting the number of times we note a topic mentioned in newspapers or magazines, on Web pages, or on radio or television broadcasts.

In short, as future-focused leaders we are constantly scanning the environment, searching for trends that might be developing. A typical comment might go something like this: "It's becoming obvious to me that technology is speeding everything up. Simply catching up isn't good enough. If we don't get ahead of the curve, we're going to be left behind."

As we analyze this hunch, we do further research. We find that virtual reality is just that—a *reality* with growing possibilities for education. Distance learning is no longer an innovation but a way to get staff and students connected with community-wide and worldwide resources. The Internet, growing at a rate of a million pages a day, is creating an unprecedented library at our fingertips. Most students have 24-hour-a-day access to that information, even at home. Biotechnology is moving forward so quickly that our science and technology teachers and labs are going to need more support to keep up. The National Science Foundation is issuing grants to pursue nanotechnology (technology at the molecular level), and scientists are talking about molecular manufacturing.

Based on our evidence and observations, we then ask, either individually or as an organization, community, or country, what the implications of this trend might be for us. If we think it deserves further attention, we gear up to deal with it.

Trend spotting is an act of scholarship, a commitment to constantly studying the environment and honing our sensitivity to what's happening around us. It is a hallmark of a connected leader.

Let's briefly analyze two of the trends listed in Figure 4.1. For each trend the analysis includes a few indications of the evidence and observations that justify the conclusion that it is a trend, followed by speculations on some of the implications for society in general and education in particular.

Trend: For the first time in history, the old will outnumber the young. (Younger → Older) (Worldwide: Developed World: Younger → Older, Underdeveloped World: Older → Younger)

Observations and Research:

- While some nations are getting dramatically older, others are getting dramatically younger.
- In 2000, 27 percent of the U.S. population was 18 or under, and 21 percent was 55 or older. By 2030, when the baby boom generation is between 66 and 84 years of age, 25 percent will be 18 or under and 30 percent will be 55 or older (U.S. Social Security Administration, 2000).
- A child born in the United States in 2001 is expected to live 29.9 years longer than a child born in 1900 (American Association of Retired Persons and Administration on Aging, 1999).

- In 1960, there were 2.37 births in the United States per 100 people. By 1990, the rate had dropped to 1.67, and in 2002 it dropped even further to 1.39 (*World Almanac and Book of Facts 2004*).
- In 2001, the United States reported 8.5 deaths per 1,000 people, compared with 14.7 in 1910 (*World Almanac and Book of Facts 2004*).
- In 1950, 16 people were working for every person drawing benefits from the U.S. Social Security system. In 1960, the ratio stood at 5 to 1. In 2000, it dropped to 3.2 to 1. By 2020, it will drop even further to 2.4 to 1. In 2040, only 2 people will be working for every person drawing benefits from the system (Burtless, 1997).

Implications for Society at Large:

- Pension programs in the United States will likely be strained to their limits as the ratio of retirees closes in on the number of actual workers contributing to pension funds.
- As baby boomers move closer to and into retirement, their political clout will increase. Seniors often have the time and inclination to vote and the life experience to make their case exceedingly convincing to decision makers.
- Communities will need to plan ahead for quality geriatric medical care, assisted living, nursing homes, geriatric day care, and other services for an aging population.
- Nostalgia for boomers will likely mean a trip down memory lane with the Rolling Stones rather than Glenn Miller.

Implications for Education:

- As generational competition increases for public funds, communities, states, and nations will need to balance the political demands of the young and the old.
- Education systems may need to recruit and retain older citizens for service as educators, because growing enrollments during the early

part of the 21st century will run squarely into massive retirements of teachers and others.

- Demand will grow for school- and community-based adult and career education, community college and four-year college and university programs, and other opportunities for lifelong learning.
- Cross-generational communication will become essential as schools and colleges focus on how to build services and maintain understanding and support across five generations.
- The ability to communicate across generations will likely become a basic skill.

Trend: Release of human ingenuity will become a primary responsibility of education and society. (Information Acquisition → Knowledge Creation and Breakthrough Thinking)

Observations and Research:

- Cognitive research generally confirms that the brain, perhaps more than anything else it does, connects information and ideas. We need to give it things to connect.
- A fresh generation of intellectual entrepreneurs is putting pieces together, seeing certain things in a whole new light, dealing with paradox and controversy, developing creative solutions to problems, and conceiving of new knowledge-based industries (Marx, 2000).
- Creativity is multidimensional and experiential, and it springs from working and thinking across disciplines (Florida, 2004).
- Understanding is growing that individuals possess multiple intelligences, and the question of whether the student should adjust to the school or the school should adjust to the student is more frequently asked (Gardner, 1993).
- At the turn of the century, knowledge workers made up about 30 percent of the U.S. workforce but accounted for about 50 percent of

total wages. "Brain-Gain cities" are engaging in "urban warfare" to attract these "creatives" (Florida, 2004, p. xxvii). If a country does not produce jobs for knowledge workers, they will move to another place in the world where they can profit from their creative genius.

Implications for Society at Large:

- Progressive communities, businesses, governmental and nongovernmental organizations, and countries will compete for creative people who will conceive of new solutions for problems, as well as generate new ideas, products, services, and whole new industries.
- People will become increasingly dismissive of pat answers and arbitrary solutions, preferring instead to consider alternatives or scenarios that result from putting divergent information and ideas together to create new knowledge.
- Those who insist on maintaining the status quo or who lack the resources to become part of an accelerating global knowledge/information age may feel left out, lose hope, become angry, and strike out at people and nations that are on a fast track.

Implications for Education:

- Education systems will be expected to apply what they've learned from cognitive research to help students learn across disciplines.
- Thinking and reasoning will be increasingly seen as basic skills.
- Educators will be expected to help students turn data and information into usable knowledge and knowledge into wisdom.
- Following classroom or online presentations or discussions, students will likely be asked, "Does what you've learned today trigger any ideas for you?"
- No matter how well managed, education institutions will be expected to demonstrate visionary, intellectual, and courageous leadership

that connects information and ideas and encourages the release of genius among students, staff, and community.

- Futures studies will likely become an essential part of education.

Why Educators Must Recognize and Respond to Trends

Trends usually emerge from societal forces that are shaking our institutions like earthquakes. Some trends are accompanied by no less than social tsunamis. Nowhere do these trends have greater impact than in our education systems, our schools and colleges.

Think about it: our schools are expected to function within the *present* (their current environments), preparing students for the *future*, not for the *past*. Those environments are changing more rapidly than ever before, driven at least in part by quantum leaps in communication, transportation, biological/medical, and other technologies.

Nothing less than a revolution is spurring these massive trends as one force affects another, all with implications for education. In a variety of ways, most trends are related, not isolated. For example, better medical care and lower birthrates lead to the aging of the population. Quantum increases in computer speed and capacity affect the way we teach and learn and sometimes leave us with a digital divide, separating the technology-rich from the technology-poor. Educators are expected to prepare students to be knowledge workers as the economy moves toward finding its primary value in social and intellectual capital. Knowledge creation and breakthrough thinking are the logical outcome of having exponentially expanding amounts of information available at our fingertips and our growing ability to connect what we know across disciplines. Scientific discoveries and societal realities force increasingly difficult ethical choices. Often, the quickening pace of change gets ahead of our tolerance for it or our willingness or ability to prepare students for life in a fast-changing world.

Just a few short years ago, when asked to identify trends, educators at many levels were likely to list immediate and persistent problems that were taking too much of their time and inhibiting their daily progress. Today, growing numbers of connected, future-focused leaders understand that societal trends are not just issues du jour.

The trick is to put on our generalist's hat—to back off and consider those forces in society that are driving the issues and, in some cases, inflaming the problems. In the process, we may discover not just problems but exciting opportunities that are also increasing exponentially.

Ultimately, how we deal with, how we shape, and even how we set trends will be an important driver in determining whether we move forward or fall backward at an unprecedented pace. The world will not wait for us.

How to Get a Handle on Trends

The very process of identifying and dealing with trends puts us in touch with the broader world and the forces buffeting every institution, including our education system and its students. Once connected, we're in a much better position both to learn from and to influence the whole of society. The following are some basic steps in the process of getting a handle on trends:

1. **Inform the discussion.** Encourage your staff and community to get involved in spotting possible trends. Ask them to read or to hear presentations about the trends discussed in this book and perhaps others. Encourage scholarship. Devote a portion of regular meetings to identifying what people consider to be possible trends. Conduct surveys. Meet with staff and community groups. Tap the genius, the thinking, of a broad range of your organization's constituency.

2. **Consider formalizing the process.** You might want to consider convening one or more trends councils, vision councils, or futures councils to engage in this type of "generative thinking." A respected and capable member of the community might even serve as chair, with meetings held a couple of times a year and a goal of helping

your organization or community keep an ear to the ground. These councils, which might have frequently rotating memberships to involve as many people as possible, would not make decisions but would be strictly advisory. The council's (or councils') insights can be helpful in planning and staying in touch with a panoply of emerging possibilities and in making even more informed decisions.

3. **Consider implications.** Individually, and in small or large groups, ask, "What are the implications of these trends for our schools, school systems, or colleges?" and "What are the implications of these trends for what our students need to know and be able to do?" Stretching the possibilities, you might engage thoughtful and diverse groups of people in thinking about the implications of these trends for science education, social studies, counseling, community education, or other fields.

4. **Broaden the scope.** Present these trends to your broader community. Take the lead in asking people both inside and outside the immediate education system to identify further implications of the trends for areas of concern such as economic growth and development, workforce development, and other concerns that will impact the overall quality of life in the community. In some cases, you might want to take the process through an additional step by identifying the implications of a few of the implications you've uncovered. For example, if an implication of the trend about aging is a realization that demand will grow for adult education and lifelong learning, what specifically will that mean for your local school system or your college or university?

5. **Set up a structure to use the wealth.** Make the process of identifying, monitoring, and considering the implications of trends part of each day's work. Also, build flexibility into the system. Be ready to adjust to a world in motion. Let everyone in on the exciting prospect of turning what might otherwise have been a static organizational plan into a living strategy.

Noted education reformer John Goodlad has cautioned, "We aren't going to create the schools of the 21st century, because no one is working at it" (Stone, 1999, p. 264). Those are fighting words from a thoughtful educator. Is he right? Knowing Goodlad, he would like nothing more than for us to prove him wrong. Football coach Vince Lombardi expressed a thought similar to Goodlad's when he said, "Failing to plan is planning to fail."

A Pivotal Opportunity for Leadership

Business and political leaders have often come together to discuss the future of education. They have convened the meetings and, in some cases, didn't even invite educators. Those who initiated the discussions believed that educators were committed only to maintaining the status quo.

When a school system, college, or university convenes its staff and community to consider the implications of an array of societal trends, it is taking an act of leadership. It is establishing itself as an institution that is the crossroads and central convening point of the community it serves.

Here's the challenge: Take the lead! It will pay off in helping keep the education system (or any other organization, for that matter) on the cutting edge, in gaining respect and building relationships community-wide, and in making sure students are getting an education that truly prepares them for the future.

Additional Trends

Moving beyond the 16 trends listed in Figure 4.1, let's branch out to trends that grew from the future-focused leadership of other education organizations. Some may be consistent with the trends just discussed. Others may take us into new territory. One of the following lists was developed by a national education organization, another by a local school system, and another by the council of advisors that contributed their ideas to this book.

Trends Identified by the Education Commission of the States

At the turn of the 21st century, the Education Commission of the States (ECS) in Denver, Colorado, published a list of educational, demographic, technological, economic, political, and social trends under the title "Future Trends Affecting Education" (Education Commission of the States, 1999). The organization made the following observations:

- Competition among schools for students, educators, and funds is increasing.
- Calls for education accountability are increasing at all levels.
- More school districts and states are contracting for education services.
- The demand for education professionals is rising.
- Minority students are beginning to form the student majority.
- School segregation is increasing.
- Disproportionate numbers of children and women are filling the ranks of the poor.
- The number of senior citizens is growing.
- Investments in technology infrastructure and equipment for schools are expanding.
- Technology increasingly is being used to change what happens in the classroom or school.
- Wealth is becoming concentrated in a shrinking elite.
- The unemployment rate does not reveal the extent of employment problems.
- The demand for technically skilled workers is high.
- The call for public accountability is increasing as taxpayers question the spending habits and policies of representative government.

- Term limits on governors and state legislators are growing more common.
- Unions are seeking new ways to be effective.
- Distrust of the federal government is rising.
- Consumer behavior is becoming driven by the desire to self-differentiate.
- More U.S. citizens are espousing the principles of simplicity and community.
- Nonprofit organizations are playing an increasingly important role in providing social services.
- New social ills are revealing the dark side of progress.

Trends Identified by a School District

Using a process similar to the one outlined in this book, the Naperville Community Unit School District 203 in the Chicago area identified internal and external trends affecting its future. In rethinking the system's beliefs, vision, and mission, Superintendent Alan Leis led educators and members of the community through a review of trends affecting the nation and the world, and then brought the process home by identifying forces directly affecting local schools. The trends they identified included the following (Naperville Community Unit School District 203, 2004):

External Trends:
- Increased federal and state accountability, including No Child Left Behind (NCLB) and the Individuals with Disabilities Education Act (IDEA)
- Requirement to meet all students' needs
- Increasing community diversity and globalization
- Increased need for students to be adept at technology
- Limited revenue options (federal, state, and local)

Internal Trends:

- Flat enrollment projections
- Aging facilities
- Staff turnover (retirements)
- Increased student needs in social-emotional areas
- Increased need to integrate students with special needs into regular classrooms
- High community expectations relative to communication, student achievement, and responsible use of funds

Trends Identified by the Council of Advisors

The 34-member advisory council that contributed to the ideas in this book (see Acknowledgments for a complete list of members) provided insights that were helpful in identifying and considering implications of the 16 trends listed in Figure 4.1. In addition to commenting about the trends on that list, members of the council had a number of other suggestions. The following are just a few of those items:

- "The combination of baby boomer demographics and current economic policy will set up a clash between the needs of those headed into retirement and the needs of young children for education and other services." —*Ted Stilwill, former director, Iowa Department of Education, Des Moines, Iowa*
- "A tendency is growing to ignore, abandon, and blame people in society who are in poverty or who suffer other unfortunate circumstances." —*James Rickabaugh, superintendent, Whitefish Bay School District, Wisconsin*
- "Early childhood education will become an expectation of communities for the public school system and not just an option." —*Kenneth Bird, superintendent, Westside Community Schools, Omaha, Nebraska*

- "The impact and long-term results of universal early childhood education in states that implement it at a quality level will increase the academic and social results for poor and minority students." —*Rosa Smith, president, the Schott Foundation and the Schott Center for Public and Early Education, Cambridge, Massachusetts*

- "We will see a slow decrease in our dependence on foreign oil and increased research on the use of alternative fuels, such as wind, solar, water, and bio-genome nanotechnologies." —*John Hoyle, professor of educational administration, Texas A&M University, College Station, Texas*

- "The automation of all information-flows throughout the economy will dramatically increase U.S. productivity and global competitiveness, but it will also eliminate millions of clerical and professional, managerial and technical jobs between now and 2020." —*David Pearce Snyder, consulting futurist, The Snyder Family Enterprise, Bethesda, Maryland*

- "China's taking over the manufacturing role means significant economic changes." —*Jane Hammond, superintendent-in-residence, Stupski Foundation, Mill Valley, California*

- "Knowledge of other cultures, other civilizations, other languages, and other religions will become increasingly important and critical." —*Radwan Masmoudi, founder and president, Center for the Study of Islam and Democracy, Washington, D.C.*

- "Through advances in neuroscience and cognitive science about the brain, knowledge will be attainable about an individual's thinking, learning, behavior, and feelings." —*Michael Silver, director and assistant professor of educational administration, Seattle University, Washington*

Considering the Long- and Short-Term Implications of Trends

The lists of trends presented in this chapter are not exhaustive. They're presented both for serious consideration and to provide examples to stimulate greater awareness. They are also intended to lead to the establishment of an ongoing process that will help each of us and our organizations stay ahead of the curve.

Take another look at the several trends introduced in this chapter. Now ask, "What are the implications of these trends, if any, for our education system or our community?" This process is valuable not only in thinking long-term, but also in considering how we're going to deal with issues that demand our attention *today*.

Many of the trends included in this chapter represent seismic shifts that are virtually sweeping across the landscape. Considering their implications will result not only in more informed decisions but also in well-earned respect as a dynamic, future-oriented leader. We ignore them at our peril.

Questions and Activities

1. Make consideration of trends a step in creating a future for your organization. Start with a reading of this chapter. Pay particular attention to the list of 16 trends. Then ask a diverse group to speculate on *the implications of those trends* for how education institutions are run and for what students need to know and be able to do. You might also engage the group in considering implications for the future of your community, for economic growth and development, or for the future of a city, county, state, or country.

2. Select three pairs of the 16 trends listed in Figure 4.1. In each case, consider the implications of one trend for the other. For example, what implications does the aging trend have for the trend devoted to competition for educators?

3. What are the characteristics of knowledge workers? Why is growth in the need for these workers important for education?

Readings

Florida, R. (2004). *The rise of the creative class*. New York: Basic Books.

Gardner, H. (1993). *Multiple intelligences: The theory in practice*. New York: Basic Books.

Goodstein, D. (2004). *Out of gas: The end of the age of oil*. New York: W. W. Norton.

Marx, G. (2005). *16 trends: Their profound impact on our future*. Arlington, VA: Educational Research Service; or Marx, G. (2000). *Ten trends: Educating children for a profoundly different future*. Arlington, VA: Educational Research Service.

Strauss, W., & Howe, N. (1991). *Generations: The history of America's future, 1584–2069*. New York: William Morrow.

Vital signs and *State of the world*. [Annual publications]. Washington, DC: Worldwatch Institute.

Wilber, K. (1996/2000). *A brief history of everything*. Boston: Shambhala.

Zollo, P. (2004). *Getting wiser to teens: More insights into marketing to teenagers*. Ithaca, NY: New Strategist Publications.

5 | Issue Management

We're tired of surprises. Couldn't we have predicted this would happen? Why weren't we in a leadership position to take advantage of this issue? It's always their agenda, never ours.

—Don Bagin, Don Ferguson, and Gary Marx (1985)

Issues are a little like the weather. We talk about them all the time. The question is, is anybody doing anything about them?

In fact, we *can* manage the issues. The other choice is to kick back and let the issues manage us. The former approach helps us set priorities and puts us in a good position to create a future. The latter is a one-way ticket to spending our time dealing with damage control and fighting fires that may not have even erupted had we been identifying, sorting, dealing with, or even raising issues in the first place. In short, issue management can help us stay in touch with our internal and external environments, and that is an essential part of effective future-focused leadership.

The term "issue management" was coined in 1976 by Howard Chase, a longtime public relations executive for companies such as General Mills, a former U.S. assistant secretary of commerce, and an educator. In a classic 1984 book titled *Issue Management: Origins of the Future,* he formulated some of the first definitions in this field. Chase noted that "an issue is an unsettled matter which is ready for decision." On the other hand, he said, "trends are detectable changes which precede issues" (p. 38). Chase (1981) defined weakness as "a propensity to defend yesterday rather than manage change" and exhorted leaders "to become managers of issues, not defense artists" (pp. 104–105).

As we move into the 21st century, issue management has become central to strategically shaping and sustaining programs, products, and services; communicating effectively; and developing an organizational reputation for openness and service. It is a prime component of any public relations, public affairs, or futuring process.

Types of Issues

An issue is a trend, condition, critical uncertainty, or wildcard, internal or external, that may, will, or does affect the successful accomplishment of our objectives. Organizing issues into various categories makes it easier to communicate about them and also can help us see relationships among issues—how one issue often affects many others.

One way to differentiate among issues is to consider their relative levels of immediacy. Such a differentiation might lead to three categories: critical issues, ongoing issues, and emerging issues.

Critical issues. We generally know critical issues when we see them. They are top-of-the-desk issues that we simply can't ignore because they have significant implications for the organization and what we're trying to accomplish. Not paying attention to critical issues can put at least some of our goals, and maybe even our credibility, on the critical list.

Ongoing issues. What can we depend on? A morbid comedian once narrowed that list to death and taxes. The fact is that some issues are ongoing. Every day we need to be concerned about student achievement, the budget, facilities, buying supplies, maintaining morale, and a host of other key issues. At times, any one of those issues, or a portion of one of them, could become critical.

Emerging issues. Hands down, emerging issues are best, because we have a better chance of managing them before they manage us. If we are constantly listening, reading, and generally sensing our environment, we'll likely be able to spot these emerging issues before they become chronic or critical. Keeping an ear to the ground is more than a cliché. It's a necessity for leadership.

Although issues vary from one industry or organization to another, most of them can also be categorized into various *domains*, such as social, technological, economic, educational, political, environmental, and demographic. Certain issues might be considered values issues. And, of course, some issues are internal, some are external, and some are both.

Putting Issue Management in Perspective

A cascade of forces might prevent us from getting every issue to tip our way. However, issue management allows us to manage our position more effectively. With an effective issue management program, we're in a better position to *set the agenda,* rather than responding to everyone else's. And setting the agenda allows education leaders—and leaders in other fields—to be less reactive and more proactive (Bagin, Ferguson, & Marx, 1985).

"Two elements capture the essence of the concept of issues management," according to Scott Cutlip, Allen Center, and Glen Broom, in *Effective Public Relations* (1994, p. 16). The first of those elements is "early identification of issues with potential impact on the organization." The second is "a strategic response designed to mitigate or capitalize on their consequences."

A finely honed issue management program, always at work, can help an organization readily understand its environment, deal with issues as they arise, and turn its strategic plan into a living strategy.

A Four-Step Issue Management Process

How often have we said it? "The process is often as important as the product." It's true. A process can provide a framework to help us engage people in thinking about nearly anything, to glean their wisdom and experience, to stimulate synergy, to make even better decisions, and to create a sense of ownership.

Responses to Issues

How should we respond to an issue? Answers might vary, depending on our internal and external environment. Rogene Bucholz (as cited in Grunig & Hunt, 1984, p. 296) points out four possible responses to policy issues:

1. Reactive—Rather than dealing with change, we simply fight it.
2. Accommodative—We consider the issue and adapt to what we know is a changing world.
3. Proactive—Rather than block change or acquiesce, we try to influence the change.
4. Interactive—As an organization constantly in touch with the environment, we are able to make regular adjustments to change.

Issue management pioneer Howard Chase (1984) identified four major steps in the issue management process:

- Issue identification
- Issue analysis
- Issue change strategy options (priority setting)
- Issue action programming

Each of these steps flows naturally into the next. First, we maintain our sensitivity to the environment, engaging diverse internal and external groups of people in brainstorming sessions that help us identify possible political, economic, social, technological, environmental, or other issues that could affect our organization and its goals. Second, we analyze each of those potential issues in light of theory, research, and our overall mission. We also consider the *probability* that the issue will become a major concern, and, if so, its possible *impact* on our future success. Third, we make initial judgments about priorities and consider strategic options for addressing the issue or for stimulating needed change. Fourth, we develop action programs to deal with the issue or clusters of issues. Action programs that emerge from the process might be put together by specific teams that are assigned to monitor and possibly serve as leaders, or "point people," on certain issues (Nagelschmidt, 1981, pp. 106–109).

Probability/Impact Matrix #1: Identifying and Sorting Issues

The Probability/Impact Matrix is central to the process of identifying and sorting issues. This simple but ingenious instrument can put us on the road to setting reasonable priorities in a world where everything seems to be commanding our attention.

Although we can use the Probability/Impact Matrix to think about issues by ourselves, its greatest value comes in using it to engage others in the process. Tapping the ideas and genius of your staff and community is essential to creating a future and to constantly maintaining the quality and integrity of an education system or any other organization. This process can help every leader, every school, every business, every governmental or nongovernmental organization, every community, indeed, every country, stay in touch with the issues. It can be used either in decision making or in scanning the environment to advise an organization on what it might consider if it hopes to stay in touch. Figure 5.1 shows an example of how the Probability/Impact Matrix might be used to lay out and sort two issues identified by a fictitious group made up of people representing education and the community-at-large.

The first issue, "Expectations are increasing much faster than resources," turned out to be highly significant. This fictitious group speculated that there is a *90 percent probability* that this item will become a major issue. They also reached a consensus opinion that if it does become a major issue, it will have a *high impact* on the system. Finally, the group agreed that this high-probability/high-impact issue should be considered *critical* and placed among the education system's *number-one priorities*.

A second issue, "What students are wearing is a significant distraction," did not elicit the same sense of urgency. The group reached consensus that

5.1				Probability/Impact Matrix for Identifying and Sorting Issues				
Critical	Ongoing	Emerging	Priority	**Issue Statement**	Probability (%)	High Impact	Medium Impact	Low Impact
X			1	Expectations are increasing much faster than resources.	90	X		
	X		3	What students are wearing is a significant distraction.	40		X	

there was only a *40 percent probability* the item would become a major issue. If it does, they concluded, it would have only *medium impact,* and they classified it as an *ongoing* issue. The group decided that it should be clustered with *priority-three* issues.

Organizing Groups to Work with the Probability/Impact Matrix

Any group can productively use the Probability/Impact Matrix to identify and sort issues. For a school, school system, community college, or university, the group might be the faculty or the entire staff. Other possibilities include the board of education or members of parent, student, business, professional, and community organizations. In some cases, an issues task force might be convened, including representatives of many groups. Keep in mind that some parts of this process can also be accomplished online or by using questionnaires distributed through regular mail. The following is an example of how to build a process for using the Probability/Impact Matrix:

1. **Dedicate agenda time at a regular meeting or convene a work session or leadership conference.** Periodically dedicate a segment of time (15 minutes to an hour) during a regular meeting of an administrative team, faculty, full staff, board, or community to identifying and sorting issues. Occasionally consider holding a special work session or broad-based "leadership conference" solely dedicated to the issues identification and sorting process.

2. **Provide copies of the matrix.** Provide each member of the group with a copy of the Probability/Impact Matrix, allowing rows for as many issues as you think might be reasonable.

3. **Organize people into working groups.** If the group has more than 10 members, consider organizing participants to work in smaller groups of 5 to 8.

4. **Appoint a leader and a recorder.** Ask someone in each group to serve as leader and perhaps someone else as a recorder.

5. **Use brainstorming techniques.** The leader should insist on brainstorming techniques and ensure that everyone contributes.

6. **Identify issues.** As the group identifies issues, they should not discuss them. The issues should simply be recorded in the center section of the matrix. Remember the observation, "The only bad idea in brainstorming is the idea not expressed." The later sorting process will separate wheat from chaff.

7. **Consider probabilities.** After a reasonable length of time, ask participants to review the list from top to bottom and reach consensus on the "probability" or "likelihood" that each of the items will become a major issue for the organization or program. Probability is expressed in a percentage. For example, an issue highly likely to become major might have 80, 90, or even 100 percent probability.

8. **Speculate on possible impact.** After identifying probabilities, instruct each group to again start at the top of the list and identify the potential impact of each issue on the organization or program. The group will reach quick consensus on whether that impact is high, medium, or low.

9. **Decide on type of issue.** Starting again at the top, have each group reach consensus on whether each of the identified items is a critical, ongoing, or emerging issue.

10. **Report to the group.** Leaders or recorders should then report to the full group, giving particular attention to those issues that came through the process as both high probability and high impact. If an issue is considered high in probability and high in impact, it's a good sign that the organization should consider how it will manage the issue before the issue manages the organization.

11. **Consider the group's collective wisdom in decision making.** The insights of a diverse group, working through this type of process, can be invaluable in making viable decisions that are sensitive to the environment and in helping create an even more sustainable future.

Activating the Probability/Impact Matrix via Mail or E-mail

Another possible approach to using the Probability/Impact Matrix to scan the environment relies on regular mail or e-mail. Start by collecting evidence of potential issues through formal research or through an informal review of articles or other sources. Jot those issues down. Then solicit additional issues by contacting people through regular mail or e-mail. Again, as appropriate, involve a diverse group of internal and external participants. You might even refer to them as an ad hoc issues advisory council or task force.

Review the information that members of the group share with you. Based on what you have collected and what has been submitted, develop issue statements and transfer them to the Probability/Impact Matrix. Again, distribute the matrix by regular mail or e-mail to the same group, asking each person to rate each issue based on its potential probability and impact and to speculate on both the type of issue it is and the priority it should receive. The results of the process will help you connect with the environment, gain from the wisdom and experience of those around you, and ultimately make better decisions.

Probability/Impact Matrix #2: Setting Priorities

After identifying and sorting possible issues, consider where each one falls within the quadrants of another sorting device, a Probability/Impact Matrix for setting priorities (Figure 5.2).

An issue that ranks *high in probability and high in impact* (upper-left quadrant) will very likely be a "driver," according to Clem Bezold of the Institute for Alternative Futures. You should be prepared for a driving issue to command your attention.

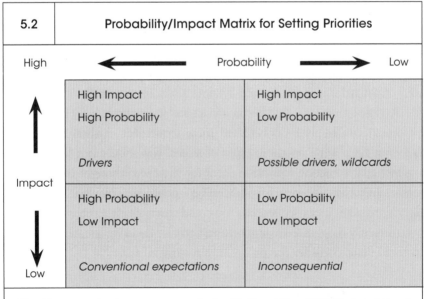

5.2	Probability/Impact Matrix for Setting Priorities	
High ←———— Probability ———→ Low		
High Impact High Probability *Drivers*	High Impact Low Probability *Possible drivers, wildcards*	
High Probability Low Impact *Conventional expectations*	Low Probability Low Impact *Inconsequential*	

Note: This matrix is based in part on concepts developed by Howard Chase (1984). The terms "drivers," "possible drivers," "wildcards," "conventional expectations," and "inconsequential issues" were part of a similar matrix used by Clem Bezold, Marsha Rhea, and Bill Rowley of the Institute for Alternative Futures in a presentation titled "Wiser Futures," during a pre-conference session at the World Future Society annual conference in San Francisco, July 18, 2003.

If an issue is *high in impact but low in probability* (upper-right quadrant), you may want to keep a file and consider whether the issue might be emerging. It is important to note that although an issue may be low in probability, wildcards or unintended consequences can seem to come out of nowhere, triggered by an unexpected event, discovery, or the proverbial "straw that broke the camel's back." John Petersen, a noted futurist and founder of the Arlington Institute in Arlington, Virginia, suggests wildcards fall into one or more of six categories: natural disasters, biomedical developments, geopolitical or sociological changes, technology and infrastructure upheaval, surprise attacks, and spiritual/paranormal events. Specifically, wildcards could include the collapse of the U.S. dollar, a worldwide move toward a noncarbon economy, or a major disruption of the information system. By anticipating wildcards, you can consider what must, can, or should be addressed; what you might prepare for; what could happen without warning; and how possible wildcard events might be changed (Petersen, 1999, pp. i–iii, 36–37).

An issue that is *low in impact but high in probability* (lower-left quadrant) can often be considered a conventional expectation. Although the issue by itself may not have what you consider a huge impact on your ability to reach your organization's goals, it could become a serious matter if not addressed.

An issue that is ranked *low in impact and low in probability* (lower-right quadrant) can likely be considered inconsequential. Although you may not even keep a file on these types of issues, you should not lose sight of the fact that someone identified them for what was thought to be a good reason. In some cases, you might even be embarrassed by what the process has identified as inconsequential. You could conclude that the issue, though not currently recognized as important, actually deserves greater attention. In that event, consider the prospect of raising an issue.

Tracking Issues

Let's assume that you've identified four issues that command attention. They will very likely come from the high probability/high impact and low probability/high impact categories. If some issues fall into the third category, low impact/high probability, you might ask, "Are we already paying attention to this issue, or do we need to get a better handle on it?"

Creating an Issue Brief

The astute issues manager—and that should be all of us—generally needs a format for getting inside an issue and tracking it over time. The format shown in Figure 5.3 can be used to create an "issue brief"—a document that records the information gathered about the issue. The issue brief itself can be kept in hard-copy format or in an organization's database.

When the collected information, or issue brief, is readily available to staff and other leaders, they can immediately address key issues with knowledge, authority, and coherence. Without something similar to the format outlined in Figure 5.3, it's possible that a lack of information will lead various people to conclude that they have little choice but to improvise. The result? The organization might give four disconnected answers to the same question. How do people react when that happens? They will likely say, "They don't have their act together!" or "They're all over the map on this issue!"

Outcomes of the Process

The *process* of bringing people together to identify and sort issues can be as important as the *product*. Here are some examples of what can happen next after issues have been identified, sorted, and tracked. The issues process can

- Inform the daily operation of the system. It can serve as an early warning system to help educators and others respond to needs and adapt to a fast-changing society. Rather than being out of touch, they will be in touch.

5.3	Format for an Issue Brief

What is the issue? Compose a brief, easy-to-understand statement of the issue. In describing the issue, make sure not to use jargon or unexplained abbreviations.

Significance of the issue to the organization. First, place a check mark to indicate whether the issue has been identified as critical, ongoing, or emerging. Note its probability percentage and potential impact. Ask "what if" questions. Then spell out at least five reasons the issue is or will be significant to the organization.

Type of Issue: ___ Critical   ___ Ongoing   ___ Emerging

Probability: ___%

Potential Impact: ___ High ___ Medium ___ Low

Reasons the issue will or could be significant:

1.

2.

3.

4.

5.

Next critical date. Determine when action on the issue might or will be taken, or when action might be expected or required. This entry might include a calendar of upcoming events or benchmarks.

Impact statement. Develop a brief, easy-to-understand statement expressing the possible impact the issue could have on the organization and its ability to reach its goals.

Current position on the issue. What is the organization's current position on this issue? Has that position changed? What are the positions of other organizations?

5.3	Format for an Issue Brief (cont.)

Background. Include details explaining the emergence and development of this issue. Craft the statement so that a person who is not informed could readily understand the explanation.

Actions to date. What actions has the organization taken to date on this issue?

Key contact person. Include the name and contact information for the person, if any, who is assigned to tracking this issue for the organization and keeping the issue brief up-to-date.

Reference material, bibliography. List any reports, memos, books, articles, Web sites, or other materials or links that would be helpful to anyone needing background information on this issue.

Plan of action. If a plan of action exists for dealing with this issue, explain it here.

- Offer a framework for individuals to consider numerous issues that might arise during a normal day's work.
- Present an opportunity to examine what is currently on the list of issues and decide either that some issues might be missing or that some don't currently deserve a prominent place on the list. Let's face it. Issues do come and go.
- Help people see relationships among issues and better understand how one issue can affect another.
- Point out blind spots or needs that can be addressed by actually raising an issue.
- Provide information that can guide the planning process of the organization, department, or program.
- Stimulate the formation of coalitions, task forces, committees, or work groups that convene, in person or online, to study and develop strategies for addressing an issue.

- Enhance policymaking to help ensure that appropriate policies are either in place or have been adjusted to deal with constantly changing realities.

Perhaps even more important, the process taps into the thinking of people, creates synergy, and promotes a sense of ownership. One outcome of the process might be a statement like this: *"I learned a lot from other people. I had a chance to present my ideas and have them seriously considered. Now I have a sense that we're all in this together. If I'm part of the process of identifying issues, then I'd better be there to help the organization deal with them."*

Another outcome of the process of identifying, sorting, and tracking issues is that it promotes a generalist view. *Internally,* the process can help us think and act across disciplines or departments. Getting diverse groups involved in the discussion is likely to make clear that issues are not necessarily isolated. One issue can affect another. In fact, taking the generalist's view, we can discover that an isolated solution could have multiple side effects, creating additional issues (both opportunities and problems) in other areas. *Externally,* the process can involve representatives from many segments of a community, an organization, or an industry. As diverse groups work together, they find that they have certain issues in common. For example, the group might decide that high-quality education is basic to nearly every aspiration a community has. A coalition might form around helping the education system get the funding and other resources it needs to get the job done. Educators, parents, older citizens, business and professional people, government representatives, and many others might then coalesce around what they have in common.

Examples of Issues

The following are examples of issues identified by three groups: an awards program of the Issue Management Council, the Education Commission of the States (ECS), and the council of advisors for this book.

W. Howard Chase Award Winners

The Issue Management Council presents an annual W. Howard Chase Award to recognize an organization's excellence in issue management. Here are some recent award winners and the issues they addressed:

- 1989—Pacific Bell Telephone Company, *Building a Public-Interest Vision*
- 1990—Society for Human Resource Management, *Implementing Issue Management to Achieve Association Goals*
- 1991—Northern States Power Company, *Acid Rain and Environmental Protection*
- 1992—NYNEX Corporation, *Customer Privacy*
- 1996—Weyerhaeuser Company, *Northern Spotted Owl*
- 1997—Prudential Insurance Company of America, *Declining Community Involvement in the United States*
- 2001—DaimlerChrysler, *"Fit for a Kid" Initiative on Child Passenger Safety*
- 2002—Eastern Idaho Regional Medical Center, *The Open Door Initiative*

Winners of the Chase Award, primarily businesses and associations, were judged on "a demonstrated commitment to systems resolution of an issue that relates to the organization's performance, senior management support for the process, cross-functional participation at many levels of the organization, a social responsibility component, and benefits that accrued to the organization, its stakeholder groups, and society at large" (Issue Management Council, n.d.).

Education Commission of the States (ECS)

ECS, located in Denver, Colorado, has identified issues and developed information to help state and other leaders address them. That information is available on the commission's Web site, http://www.ecs.org.

Among K–12 issues identified by ECS (2003) are the following: assessment, brain research, class size, closing the achievement gap, economic/workforce development, education research, extended-day programs, finance, gifted and talented, governance, international education, kindergarten, language arts, leadership, No Child Left Behind, school size, special education, standards, student records/rights, uniforms/dress codes, vocational education, and vouchers.

Postsecondary issues identified by ECS (2003) include the following: academic issues, access, admissions, adult learning/continuing education, affordability, community colleges, competition, disabled students, distance learning/virtual university, economic/workforce development, employment, equity, minority/diversity issues, outreach, P–16, remediation, and teacher quality.

The Council of Advisors

The Creating a Future Council of Advisors that responded to a questionnaire specifically for this book identified nearly 100 issues facing education. The categories of issues identified by the council included the following: accountability, achievement, curriculum, demographics, diversity, early childhood education, equity, facilities, finance/funding, flexibility, health, higher education, infrastructure, international/global concerns, leadership, learning, No Child Left Behind, the pace of change, policy, poverty, public support, the purpose of education, relevancy of preparation programs, respect, special education/special needs, specialization, staffing, standards, student issues, teacher issues, technology, and testing and assessment.

The following 10 issue statements represent just a sampling of the council's contributions. (See additional examples in Appendix A.) In reviewing these issues, consider whether they are critical, ongoing, or emerging. What is the probability or likelihood that each will become a major issue for your school, district, or organization—10 percent, 50 percent, 90 percent? If it currently is or later becomes a major issue, how would you describe its potential impact—high, medium, or low? What priority should this issue have as you develop your plans—priority 1, priority 2, or priority 3? What plans of action should you pursue as an individual, as a community, as a nation, or as a world to deal with these issues?

- "Early childhood initiatives for children in poverty are receiving unprecedented political attention and should rise to the top of the agenda in the very near future. Educators need to take advantage of the current high level of attention given to early childhood education initiatives so that badly needed programs can be funded, especially in high-poverty areas." —*Carol G. Peck, president and CEO, Rodel Foundation, Scottsdale, Arizona, and a veteran school superintendent*

- "The inability to definitively establish what educational strategies are effective for children 5 to 18 years of age in elementary and secondary schools is stymieing progress. The connection between a person's present and future life and what is going on in education is almost nonexistent. Hence, there is a lack of goals, directions, and paths to those goals driven by education." —*Joseph F. Coates, president, Consulting Futurist, Inc., Washington, D.C.*

- "Leadership (principals, teachers, superintendents, boards of education, legislators) . . . lacks the required focus, courage, and will for these difficult times. Circumstances require a very special 'stand and deliver' kind of leadership from everyone to make decisions on students' behalf." —*Rosa Smith, president, Schott Foundation and Schott Center, Cambridge, Massachusetts, and a veteran school superintendent*

- "Poor children, children of color, and children for whom English is not a first language remain seriously disadvantaged relative to their more affluent, white, native-English-speaking peers. This comes at a time when the standards defining a good education leading to satisfactory economic, social, and personal levels of performance are becoming more rigorous, not less. The nation is sinking into a moral morass as we become hardened to the conditions we are creating for the most vulnerable in our society. Those with the characteristics of the disadvantaged today will constitute a majority of the country within two generations. Given these facts, both the nation's soul and economy are at risk." —*David Hornbeck, former president and CEO, International Youth Foundation, Baltimore, Maryland, a veteran state and local superintendent of schools, and currently president, the Children's Defense Fund*

- "The unwillingness of schools to address language diversity is short-sighted and foolish. Language diversity is actually lower now than it was at the beginning of the 20th century, but strategies for coping with it are weaker. In addition, those described as 'minorities' are not that in any meaningful statistical sense—even at the state level in many parts of the country. They are certainly not minorities in the communities where they live. We ought, for example, to stop thinking of Spanish as a 'foreign language.' It is one of several principal languages of the United States." —*Douglas Greenberg, president and CEO, Survivors of the Shoah Visual History Foundation, Los Angeles, California*

- "Reducing or eliminating arts and humanities programs from the curriculum is a danger. We want well-rounded kids . . . but we demand curriculums that feature depth over breadth. The success of our schools will be measured on how quickly we move toward emphasizing the development and application of each individual's skills and talents, as opposed to being an informational delivery system. If we continue to look for silver bullets or quick fixes, then the educational pendulum will continue to swing wildly to and fro." —*George Hollich, retired director of curriculum and summer programs, Milton Hershey School, Hershey, Pennsylvania*

- "Elected officials, policymakers, and the general public lack the political will to provide the support, resources, and civic commitment to demand that *all* children have access to and receive a quality public education. Institutional issues and challenges will *not* be resolved by the usual 'reading to your child' missive (although that is important), but by leadership that uses community and democratic processes as the key instruments of action. Ron Heifitz calls this 'giving the work back to the people.' The choice for this next generation of citizens, then, is not to choose an individual school by using vouchers, but for citizens to exercise political options that act and converge on public schools that are not performing, and support and sustain those schools that do. Leaders who articulate this kind of 'civic choice' will be the Rosa Parks of public schools, not tolerating anymore a group of kids who are currently riding at the back of the educational bus. By appealing to the best in us, rather than to our avarice or self-interests, public education will once again be recognized as the great equalizer, and will also be understood to be the most powerful institution for maintaining homeland security and the national defense." —*Arnold Fege, president, Public Advocacy for Kids, Annandale, Virginia*

- "Maturing information technology has the capacity to substantially increase the educational productivity of teacher-mediated, classroom-based public schools. But this will require the redesign of traditional learning processes and the reconceptualization of the classroom instructor." —*David Pearce Snyder, consulting futurist, The Snyder Family Enterprise, Bethesda, Maryland*

- "School buildings are deteriorating, and property-poor school districts are reluctant to pass bonds and raise taxes. We will see greater involvement by government, business, and private foundations in building schools. The shared responsibility for education is the only hope for schools and the thousands of low-income families in urban and rural America." —*John Hoyle, professor of educational administration, Texas A&M University, College Station, Texas*

- "Students in the United States and internationally lack understanding of the need to have a more global perspective, with greater understanding of international issues and developments. American and international students need to have a more global perspective. The globe has truly become a village, and what happens thousands of miles away has impact and repercussions on our lives, our security, and our happiness." —*Radwan Masmoudi, founder and president, Center for the Study of Islam and Democracy, Washington, D.C.*

Issue Management: An Ongoing Process

Issue management is not a "once and you're done" process. It is, in fact, ongoing. It's a process that enables leaders to get connected by engaging people and putting their ideas, concerns, and ingenuity to work. It's also a way of thinking—a way of moving from a strategic plan to a living strategy. If we hope to *function* strategically, then we need to *think* strategically.

Questions and Activities

1. Using the Probability/Impact Matrix, involve a diverse group in identifying issues and then speculating on their potential probability and impact. At that point, identify the issue type and consider the priority it should be assigned. Also, determine those issues for which you'll develop issue briefs.
2. Consider allocating a portion of agenda time to asking that participants draw from their own recent knowledge or experience to identify critical, ongoing, or emerging issues.
3. Develop a set of issues and ask that a diverse group sort them using the Probability/Impact Matrix.
4. How would you define "an issue"?

Readings

Chase, W. H. (1984). *Issue management: Origins of the future*. Stamford, CT: Issue Action Publications.

Grunig, J. E., & Hunt, T. (1984). *Managing public relations (pp. 296–297)*. New York: CBS College Publishing.

6

More Tools and Techniques for Scanning the Environment

We are all time travelers on a journey into the future. However, we are not tourists accompanied by a guide who can tell us just what lies ahead and will keep us safe and comfortable. Instead, we are explorers in an unknown and dangerous region that no one has ever seen before.

—*Edward Cornish (2004)*

Edward Cornish, founder and longtime president of the World Future Society (WFS), is a leading proponent of environmental scanning. He urges us to "identify and understand those phenomena or aspects of the world that are most relevant to the people or groups who need this information for important decisions" (2004, p. 81).

We have a choice. We can choose to fly blind through a thick fog, or we can turn on our radar to penetrate that hazardous haze and get a clearer picture of the terrain below and the storm ahead. That's what environmental scanning does. It serves as our radar and helps us navigate the unknown rather than being unmercifully tossed by the winds or lost in a collision we might have avoided—or at least prepared for.

In Chapters 4 and 5, we took an in-depth look at identifying, analyzing, and dealing with trends and issues. In this chapter, we explore additional ways to get and stay in touch with the world around us. Despite their obvious value, these tools and techniques should not become an excuse for "shuffling things around rather than thinking," cautions veteran futurist Joseph F. Coates, coauthor of *2025: Scenarios of U.S. and Global Society Reshaped by Science and Technology.* He recommends constantly asking, "What does this mean to us?" (Coates, 2002).

The actual scanning might involve questionnaires and interviews, scholarly research, data collection, audits, focus groups, and other types of meetings or conferences. Some form of a Delphi process (described later in this chapter) and the use of brainstorming techniques and polling can help bring it all to life.

The following tools have several origins, and using them doesn't have to be a complicated process. What is complicated is working ourselves out of a situation we didn't see coming because we weren't paying attention to our internal and external environment.

PEST (Political, Economic, Social, and Technological Factors) Analysis

The PEST analysis is among the most commonly used environmental scanning tools. Although some choose to call it STEP instead of PEST, the aim is the same: to identify or predict political, economic, social, and technological factors that will affect an organization, possibly by certain points in time.

These factors are often macroenvironmental in nature, and the organization may have little direct control over them. However, not anticipating them can leave people and institutions even more vulnerable to wildcards, keep them from adapting to a changing world, and ensnare them in an ongoing state of damage control.

Political forces might involve government policies or regulations and legal issues. *Economic* forces could include variations in interest or inflation rates, economic cycles, and the cost of resources we might need. *Social* forces often relate to cultural or demographic issues, social mobility, changes in lifestyles, fashion, living conditions, attitudes about education, or other factors that affect how people think, work, and live every day. *Technological* forces could include innovations in communication, transportation, medical practice, and other areas affected by scientific and technical developments;

a growing ease in connecting and sharing information with people in many parts of the world; an acceleration in the pace of change; and shorter life cycles for existing hardware or software (FOLIO, 2004).

The PEST analysis process involves steps that may include the following:

- **Consulting** with or interviewing experts in several fields to obtain their views about these societal forces.
- **Reviewing** news media reports, results of opinion polls, and professional or trade literature for additional clues.
- **Conducting** basic research, such as obtaining demographic information and forecasts from the U.S. Census Bureau and comparing past, present, and projected information about employment and careers from the Bureau of Labor Statistics.
- **Convening** a diverse group of people, possibly representing education, business, government, and other fields. (The process could also take place as part of a regularly scheduled meeting or conference.) After participants are given an opportunity to take an in-depth look at what has been identified so far, they might be asked to provide further insights. For example, they could brainstorm what effects these forces might have on the organization, share ideas about possible actions, and recommend further sources of information.

Obviously, the PEST analysis process for scanning the environment can be used in many ways, ranging from meetings and face-to-face interviews to written and online questionnaires. It can also serve as a first step in identifying trends and issues. For example, Figure 6.1 shows partial results of a PEST analysis conducted by the Pennsylvania School Boards Association (PSBA). The PSBA board and executive/management staff completed the analysis as part of their visioning process during a retreat in 2003 to develop a new mission statement and goals for the organization.

Even groups not directly involved in education often identify education as an issue in a PEST analysis. For example, at a workshop for the Council of Manufacturing Associations, participants identified the following trends, among others, as they went through the PEST analysis process:

6.1	Partial Results of a PEST Analysis by the Pennsylvania School Boards Association

Political Forces
- Increased influence of federal and state governments on public education
- Dealing with conservative versus liberal extremes
- Public disengagement, exemplified by a decline in voter turnout

Economic Forces
- Competition for the tax dollar
- State income tax versus property tax
- Senior citizen needs versus student needs
- Brain drain
- Manufacturing jobs going overseas
- Distribution of funding among rural, urban, and suburban schools
- School construction and renovation

Social Forces
- School districts expected to be social agencies that fix all of society's ills
- Cultural conflicts and biases about education
- An aging population
- Demand for lifelong learning
- Technologically enhanced, disposable society
- Litigious, "sue me" society
- Instant gratification and the expectation of having needs met NOW
- Safety and security
- Origins of children's values

Technological Forces
- Speed of change
- Information overload
- Need for and availability of accurate information
- Need for futurists' perspectives
- Access to learning beyond the classroom
- Challenge of staying ahead of the curve

Source: Pennsylvania School Boards Association; selected comments from board, representatives, and executive/management staff during the strategic planning process, August 7–8, 2003. Used with permission.

Political—changes in trade laws; *economic*—globalization; *social*—changes around educational attainment and workforce development; and *technological*—how manufacturers operate and how their associations relate to their members (*Alternative Futures, 2003*).

STEEPV Analysis

Taking the PEST analysis a step further, Clem Bezold, Marsha Rhea, and William Rowley (2003) of the Institute for Alternative Futures in Alexandria, Virginia, suggest a STEEPV analysis—an analysis of *social, technological, economic, environmental,* and *political* factors, as well as *values.* Such an environmental scan should cause an organization to "think systematically so as not to miss important issues" and to read the "macroenvironment." "We need to recognize that everything is connected to everything else," Bezold told a July 2003 World Future Society pre-conference session devoted to "Wiser Futures." He also suggested considering these factors in understanding the "operating environment, ranging from an entire industry to a single organization."

As in the PEST analysis, interviews, opinion polls, literature searches, news media reports, and basic research can help to inform STEEPV. Sharing hard data or findings might help move the process a step beyond the "observation" stage, although observations by a diverse group of people are an important part of the process. Figure 6.2 shows hypothetical examples of observations and data emerging from an education institution's use of this process to identify factors that might, will, or already do affect the organization and its mission.

Stretching this process a bit further, we could ask a diverse group to take part in a STEEPED analysis—to help us identify the *social, technological, economic, environmental, political, educational,* and *demographic* forces affecting the entire community. If we consider an education system to be the crossroads and central convening point for a community, then taking that kind of initiative is a far-reaching and future-oriented act of leadership.

By identifying these dynamic forces, participants are likely to see the connection between high-quality education and nearly everything else that happens throughout the community.

Gap Analysis

Perhaps no other approach to environmental scanning so directly connects the present with potential futures as gap analysis. The process asks participants to identify 10 to 20 characteristics of the ideal organization and to compare those "ideals" with current realities, perhaps on a scale of

6.2	Hypothetical Example of a STEEPV Analysis

Social Factors
- The average age in our community has increased from 38 in 1995 to 48 in 2005.
- Enrollment in our school system has dropped 15 percent during that same 10-year period.

Technological Factors
- Computer speed and capacity are doubling every 18 months.
- Upgrades of the district's computer system are two years behind because of a lack of funding.

Economic Factors
- Although consumer spending has increased, tax collections and allocations will be delayed for at least a full year.
- One business employing 100 people in our community closed last year, and the Industrial Development Council is seeking to at least replace it.

Environmental Factors
- The community is committed to maintaining the quality of the air, water, land, and other aspects of the physical environment.
- In considering the learning environment, a climate survey and a separate study of physical facilities indicated that staff will need more focused professional development and that one-half of the district's schools will require structural and aesthetic improvements.

6.2	Hypothetical Example of a STEEPV Analysis (cont.)

Political Factors

- Most members of the school board were elected because of their commitment to shaping schools capable of preparing students for the future.
- During the most recent elections, 60 percent of those elected to the state legislature referred to education as "an expense," whereas 40 percent referred to education as "an investment."

Values

- In a recent survey conducted by the school system, "caring, quality, integrity, service, and social responsibility" were among the highest-ranking values descriptors identified by staff.
- In another recent survey, 85 percent of parents and the community said they preferred the statement, "Education should prepare students for the future as good citizens and as employable, well-adjusted people," compared with 15 percent who preferred the statement, "The purpose of education is to ensure that students pass required achievement tests on those subjects that are assessed."

1 to 5. That comparison helps us discover gaps between where we are and where we would like to be. We can then move forward to fill the gaps and periodically repeat the process. Figure 6.3 is a hypothetical example of a form used to conduct a gap analysis around the question of how flexible a school district is in developing curriculum.

Root Cause, Defining Moments, Historical Analysis

Certain events represent defining moments in the life of an organization. These are "events that have social consequences, and they are known and experienced by large groups of people," according to Geoffrey Meredith, Charles Schewe, and Janice Karlovich in *Defining Markets, Defining Moments* (2002, p. xvii).

Arguably, some events or actions that can bring substantial benefits or consequences may have involved only a few individuals. A case could be made that the ethical indiscretions of firms such as ENRON and World-Com at the turn of the 21st century were known to only a few until their consequences became known to many.

Herb Rubenstein, CEO of Growth Strategies, Inc., refers to these types of industrywide events as "inflection points and more particularly situations within an organization's history when some key decision was made or invention was created that reflected the organization's core values or demonstrated the true character of the organization or its personnel" (2000, p. 7).

In a special report titled "The Art of Foresight," the World Future Society notes that futurists might "study historical events in order to

6.3	Hypothetical Gap Analysis Form

Operative Question: How flexible is the organization in developing and adopting new curriculum?

Current Situation: Adoption of new curriculum takes a minimum of 18 months.

Characteristic/Ideal/Alternative Future: The curriculum development process should help the system meet basic requirements and yet be flexible enough to quickly adapt to the needs of a fast-changing world.

Identifying the Gap: On a scale of 1 to 5, with 5 being closest and 1 being furthest from the ideal, how would you rate the organization as it currently exists? (Circle your choice.)   1   2   3   4   5

What should we do to close the gap between where we are and where we want to be? Please share your opinion in one or two sentences.

_____

_____

_____

_____

anticipate the outcome of current developments. Often, a current situation can be compared to one or more situations in history that seem to be similar" (2004, p. 35).

These various observations come together in a process called "root cause, defining moments, historical analysis." This type of analysis sometimes gets under way when a diverse group of people with knowledge of the organization are asked to consider a manageable number of present situations, both favorable and unfavorable. In some cases, the discussion might focus on a single situation. Together, members of the group identify decisions made or conditions that existed in the past that might have led to the current set of circumstances. Rubenstein (2000) suggests use of a "tree-like" graphic structure, laying out the assumptions at the bottom of a diagram and the end result at the top. This tool can also be used to consider root causes and defining moments that might be created to stimulate a *desired* future.

Figure 6.4 shows a hypothetical example of a school system's use of this tool. If the example were laid out in Rubenstein's "tree" graphic, the "Situation" would be the above-ground portion of the tree and the "Possible Root Causes or Defining Moments" would be the below-ground portion.

Flexibility/Innovation Analysis

"Often, the ability of a company or nonprofit organization to compete successfully rests with its ability to be flexible and innovate rapidly," according to Herb Rubenstein (2000, pp. 9–10), who played a key role in developing this fresh approach to analyzing the environment. Educators have every right to be proud of the fact that they provide a vital service. They also create value that tax or tuition payers must be willing to support. Therefore, in a fast-changing world, they have no choice but to follow Rubenstein's advice and be flexible and innovative.

The process that drives this type of analysis might include the following steps:

- **Identify major activities of the organization.** Also consider the component parts of each major activity. For example, teaching is a primary activity of an education system, but what are the numerous other activities that could contribute to a teacher's success or failure?
- **Convene a diverse group to be directly involved in the flexibility/ innovation analysis.** Identify ideals. Members of this group should be objective, familiar with the organization, and able to develop a

6.4	Hypothetical Example of a Root Cause and Defining Moments Analysis

Situation: In the last two elections, a measure to override a state-imposed tax cap has failed to pass. The financial situation for the school district is critical, yet a recent opinion poll indicated that only 35 percent of voters would support an override proposal this coming year.

Possible Root Causes or Defining Moments:

- Four years ago, the district announced that defeat of an override proposal would result in fewer activity programs for students. Even though the proposal was defeated, activity programs were retained.
- Two years ago, the district, facing an even more serious financial situation, warned that the number of students per teacher would be increased by two unless the override was passed. Although a number of essential investments in facilities, new curriculum, professional development, and technology were delayed, the pupil-teacher ratio was maintained.
- Only 25 percent of homes in the district have children in school.
- The district's communication is directed primarily at staff of the school system and parents of students.
- When the district announces its budget or override proposals, it refers to "expenses" rather than "investments that will pay off for our community."
- A local manufacturing company has just closed its plant and laid off 200 workers.
- A recent economic slump and a drop in interest rates have reduced the amount of spendable income available to retirees.
- The district faces challenges in credibility and communication.

series of statements reflecting the ideal for flexibility and innovation. Those statements could apply to parts of the organization and the organization as a whole.

- **Rate the organization's flexibility and potential for innovation.** When statements have been developed describing the ideal, ask members of the group, or perhaps even an expanded group, to rate each one according to the organization's flexibility or willingness to innovate. A 1-to-10 scale might work well, with 10 being most flexible and willing.

- **Review the results of the analysis and decide what to do next.** Based on the analysis, the organization might consider how it can become more flexible and innovative. A low score on any of the statements could be an indication that the organization needs to let go and become more interested in pursuing new ideas or be left in the dust.

Figure 6.5 shows a hypothetical example of a form used to conduct a flexibility/innovation analysis.

SWOT Analysis

Like all the other scanning tools mentioned in this chapter, a SWOT (*strengths, weaknesses, opportunities,* and *threats*) analysis can be used at any level—from a department or organization to an industry or profession, from a local community to a state, province, or nation. Often, a review of strengths, weaknesses, opportunities, and threats comes near the end of the scanning processes, because other scans, such as trends, issues, or gap analysis might be helpful in enriching the SWOT discussion.

What techniques can an organization use to pursue a SWOT analysis? Here are several suggestions:

- **Conduct** other processes for scanning the environment and review findings.

- **Convene** a thoughtful and diverse group of staff, board members, community members, students, suppliers, and perhaps other constituents to help identify strengths, weaknesses, opportunities, and threats. (Another possibility is distribution of a written or online questionnaire.)
- **Consider** driving questions such as these (Manktelow, 2005): What do we do well? What do others see as our strengths? What could we do better? What are the opportunities or resources that could be available to us? What obstacles do we face? Is demand for the services we provide changing? Do we have consistent funding sources? What could actually threaten our existence?

Let's take a closer look at what we might discover through SWOT analysis. The following items represent just a few possibilities, but they are

6.5	Example of a Flexibility/Innovation Analysis

Instructions: Please rate each statement on a scale of 1 to 10, based on how accurately it describes our education system. (Circle your choice.)

Statement	Low → High
The organization would welcome an ongoing process for creating a future to keep pace with a fast-changing world.	1 2 3 4 5 6 7 8 9 10
The organization is eager to constantly define who its stakeholders are.	1 2 3 4 5 6 7 8 9 10
The organization strives to obtain and effectively use state-of-the-art technology.	1 2 3 4 5 6 7 8 9 10
The organization is willing to take risks that are essential to eventual success for the education system and for students.	1 2 3 4 5 6 7 8 9 10

typical of the types of items identified by groups of people who take part in the process:

- **Strengths** will likely cover organizational readiness; reputation; vision; staff knowledge, talents, experience, connections, and willingness; organizational culture; technical capabilities; community and political support; cohesiveness; and how well the organization's policies, programs, and activities align with its mission.

- **Weaknesses** might reveal shortcomings in any of the items considered in assessing strengths. For example, the program may be aligned with the mission, but the mission may not be appropriate for the future. Many organizations might also consider where they stand in the competitive environment. Other weaknesses could include staff that is spread too thin, lack of technology, inappropriate facilities, funding issues, or a lack of diversity.

- **Opportunities** have very likely been identified, or at least suggested, in considering the implications of societal trends or in describing the characteristics of an organization poised for the future. A good approach is to identify a constellation of opportunities and then consider each of them in terms of whether it is short- or long-term, its potential effectiveness for helping achieve success, and the possibilities it holds for responding to needs and building public support. Typical opportunities might include availability of research, access to legislators or other government leaders, growing support for needed programs or facilities, and the possibility of engaging staff and the community in the process of creating a future.

- **Threats** could be posed by political, economic, social, or technological forces. They might reveal emerging criticism or the possible birth of pressure groups, budget shortfalls, unreasonable requirements, and a world moving too fast for the organization to accommodate. Identifying threats should help us objectively consider what might need to be done to deal with them, not simply create a culture of paranoia. On the positive side, threats could also represent growing discomfort with the status quo and further energize us to create the organization of the future. Some threats might include a weak economy, competition for resources or attention, unfunded mandates, and a sense that success has led to complacency.

Some advise caution in using SWOT. Try not to exaggerate the strengths, weaknesses, opportunities, and threats either positively or negatively. Use the process, but be reasonable.

Additional Environmental Scans

The Delphi Process

One of the most versatile ways to probe thinking and move toward consensus is the Delphi process. This practical approach to collecting data and good ideas can be used as part of many forms of environmental scanning.

The Delphi process, named for the Greek Delphic oracle and her reputed skills in interpretation and foresight, is a product of work done in the 1950s by the Rand Corporation. It was, and still is, seen as a way to obtain reliable consensus among a group of experts using questionnaires and controlled feedback and to get a handle on possible future events.

Although the purist will likely tell you that you must precisely follow all steps in the process, a modified Delphi can also be very helpful. A pure Delphi advocate will likely insist on at least a three-round series of questionnaires. Others might feel a two-round process is sufficient. To use the Delphi process, follow these steps:

1. **Appoint an expert panel.** The panel might include a group of people with expertise in many areas but with a common interest in education, for example. Panel members will respond to questionnaires independently and will not know the identities of other panelists.
2. **Distribute a round-one questionnaire.** The initial questionnaire asks members of the panel to individually express opinions on an

issue in question. For example, you might ask them to identify trends likely to affect society during the next 10 years.

3. **Distribute a round-two questionnaire.** For the second round, construct a questionnaire that includes each of the items submitted by all members of the group in round one. Ask the same respondents to rank each of the items on a scale, such as 1 to 5 or 1 to 9, and to provide any comments they would like to share on any or all of the items. You might also ask respondents to suggest additional items that they think are important but don't find on the list.

4. **Distribute a round-three questionnaire.** In round three, develop a questionnaire that includes each of the items ranked and listed in light of the results of round two. Consider including any additional items that were submitted. In other words, feed the results of round two back to the same group for review and further comment. In round three, you might ask members of the group to speculate on the likelihood that the trend, issue, or concern will develop, and if so, its potential impact—high, medium, or low.

5. **Review the results of the process.** Summarize the results of the Delphi process in a report. Sections of the report might be devoted to each item, pointing out the level of support it had from the group and including the gist of participants' comments. If some members of the group express extreme views compared with the group median, consider whether to do individual interviews to fully understand their opinions. A fourth-round questionnaire could also be an option.

6. **Share and consider using the results.** The process of sharing results can vary, though typically the findings are shared with members of the panel, along with a note of thanks. In addition, you might announce the results publicly or simply use the results as part of a decision-making or planning process.

The Delphi process has both advantages and disadvantages. Delphi advocates note that the process provides a way for getting people with views that often conflict to balance those views against a group. Because respondents work anonymously and independently, not as a committee, the process is more likely to avoid dominance by one person or group over another. It also saves those who think they might represent a minority position from losing face.

Drawbacks of the Delphi process include the time it takes to compose, complete, and tabulate the questionnaires. Some overcome that concern by keeping the questionnaires as short as possible and by reducing the number of rounds from three to two (Kerr, 2001).

Other Scanning Tools

Some organizations use **stakeholder analysis** to identify people and organizations that currently have a stake in what they do and those who should have a stake, and to help determine how to inform or involve each of them. **Competitive analysis** helps organizations get a better idea about those who might be in competition with them, what the competition is doing and how they are doing it, what the competition might do in the future, and the potential impact the competition might have on the organization. Appendix C presents an example of an index that combines several factors used to get a reading on the "state of the future." It might be interesting to consider what factors would be included in developing a **State of Education Index.**

The list of tools and techniques for environmental scans included in this chapter is not exhaustive. In fact, it should be considered not just as a source of possible scanning methods but also as an idea-jogger. Use it to stimulate thinking about other approaches to getting a better handle on the internal and external environment.

The Importance of the Process

"The process is as important as the product!" An exaggeration? Often! However, simply developing a list of facts or possibilities without a process that captures the thinking of others, internally and externally, can come up short. A legitimate process or combination of processes, such as those noted in this chapter, can stimulate the creative and future-oriented thinking of a few, a dozen, a hundred, or even more people. Involvement in the process can also lead to a greater sense of ownership, which will likely be critical to ultimate success.

Questions and Activities

1. Review the processes described in this chapter. Select three to six of them for use in regularly scanning the environment. Briefly explain why you chose the processes that you did.

2. Use combinations of the processes described in this chapter, not only to help you develop your strategic plan, but also to help you turn any plan into a living agenda by constantly staying close to the environment.

3. Consider how you could use some version of the Delphi process to enhance decision making.

4. Review the State of the Future Index found in Appendix C. What factors would you include if you were developing a State of Education Index?

Readings

Bennis, W., & Goldsmith, J. (2003). *Learning to lead: A workbook on becoming a leader* (3rd ed.). New York: Basic Books.

Coates, J., Mahaffie, J., & Hines, A. (1996). *2025: Scenarios of U.S. and global society reshaped by science and technology.* Greensboro, NC: OakHill Press.

Cornish, E. (2004). *Futuring: The exploration of the future.* Bethesda, MD: World Future Society.

The Futurist Magazine. [regular issues]. Bethesda, MD: World Future Society.

Gibson, R. (Ed.). (2002). *Rethinking the future*. London: Nicholas Brealey Publishing.

Meredith, G. E., & Schewe, C. D., with Karlovich, J. (2002). *Defining markets, defining moments*. New York: Hungry Minds.

Rubenstein, H. (1999). *Breakthrough, Inc.: High growth strategies for entrepreneurial organizations*. London: Financial Times/Prentice-Hall.

PART 3

Creating a Vision of the Future

Vision is one of the "five realities of paradigm change" identified by education consultants and authors Charles Schwahn and William Spady in their book *Total Leaders* (1998). In an article for *Principal Leadership* magazine, Spady and Schwahn declare that those realities are purpose, vision, ownership, capacity, and support. They define vision as "the clear, concrete picture of what you want your organization to look like when accomplishing its purpose and operating at its absolute or ideal best" (Spady & Schwahn, 2001).

In this part, we consider the value of history and of thinking about information and ideas that flow from environmental scans, exploring aspirations, pondering values, and meeting with others to envision and describe a preferred future. Following such an effort, we can courageously consider audacious goals that "challenge the organization to go beyond the limits of current realities and achieve its highest aspirations" (Bezold, Rhea, & Rowley, 2003).

7 | Characteristics: Identifying What We Want to Become

Ask yourself, "What is it that keeps me awake at night?"

—*Peter Schwartz (1995)*

"We need to change," the boss exhorts. "We need to do things differently. What we're doing isn't working. We need to get off the dime."

The boss might be right. However, this type of frontal command probably leads to more defensiveness than enthusiasm. The reactions might go something like this: "Change? Are you telling me I haven't been doing a good job? How will this affect what I do? What kind of change are you talking about?"

Creating a future should be an exciting process that brings people together in common purpose. Whose future will it be? Your future? My future? Or will it be *our* future? Getting together to identify the characteristics of the school system, university, business, community, country, or world we want to become can create a situation that replaces defensiveness with enthusiasm and a sense of ownership.

Identifying the Driving Question
and Getting Answers

A basic question will drive the process of determining the characteristics of the organization that we envision. That's why identifying that question is among the first steps to take. Consider the following examples of driving questions:

- What are the characteristics of a school or education system capable of preparing students for life in a global knowledge/information age?
- What are the characteristics of the education system we envision by [year]? How would we like to have people describe us?

Moving beyond education, the driving question might be this: What are the characteristics of the [country, state/province, community, city, business, profession, industry, or other organization or institution] we want to become?

Getting the answers to questions such as these involves asking some additional questions: Who should be involved? How should we engage people in the process?

Determining who should be involved is one of the first tasks to address, and additional questions can help the process. You might ask questions such as these: Who will be affected by our decisions? Whose advice or support do we need to be successful? Who has the information and experience we need to clearly build our road to the future? Should we involve staff? Should we engage a broad and diverse cross-section of the community? If we're an education system, should we involve teachers; administrators; support staff; board members; parents; nonparent taxpayers; business, government, community, and professional leaders; and others? If we're a business, should we consider involving staff, customers, suppliers, neighbors, and stockholders, as well as others who have a stake in the organization's future? What combination will give us the insights we need as we move toward creating a vision of the future?

Engaging people in the process of describing an organization of the future will begin with some basic decisions about format. Again, questions can help frame the decisions. For example, you might ask: Should we begin and end the identification process by holding one meeting of a highly diverse group? Should we ask an inclusive group to respond to a questionnaire that is distributed by a postal/delivery service or e-mail? Should we decentralize the process, using it at the school, departmental, or community level? Should we consider some combination of all of the above?

One Possible Process

When it comes to a process for identifying the defining characteristics of an organization of the future, one size doesn't fit all. Nonetheless, the following are possible steps in a process for engaging people in the task.

1. Identify a Council and Give It a Name

If you're focusing on preparing students for life in the 21st century, you might call it the Council of 21. If you are School District Number 55, you could refer to it as the Council of 55. Rather than including a significant number, consider giving the group a name such as Futures Council or Visioning Council. The name you select should have symbolic meaning that reflects your forward-looking intentions and the energy you bring to this effort. As a leader, you could actually call for the selection of more than one council. One will likely draw participants from the entire organization. Others could work at the departmental or community level.

2. Recruit a Universally Respected and Admired Honorary Chair

The honorary chair of the council should be of such stature that if she invites other community leaders to a meeting, they will find it difficult to decline. This person symbolizes the importance, seriousness, and integrity of this future-focused effort. Having at least some distance from the organization but a great deal of familiarity with its work and its importance will help ensure a sense of objectivity. It's best if this person does not have a built-in bias for the status quo or, on the other hand, an ax to grind.

To get this universally respected and admired person on board, you'll need to be clear that most of the day-to-day work will be done by staff and energetic volunteers and that the council's ideas and recommendations are advisory. This is not a decision-making group. Instead, it is a group that enlightens the visioning process through generative thinking.

If possible, the honorary chair should be apprised of the important mission of the project and engaged in discussions about the fine-tuning of the process.

3. Select a Significant Venue for the Council Meeting

Where the council meets also has symbolic value. Although school cafeterias and hotel meeting rooms are acceptable, the council's work will be even more highly regarded if the gathering takes place at a historic venue. Possibilities include legislative chambers, governor's mansions, historic homes, museums, and parks. Of course, from a practical standpoint, you'll need to have enough space, appropriate meeting room technology, and the capacity to break into small and large groups. An alternative to an actual meeting is to develop a process for gathering the council's ideas online or through regular mail.

4. Schedule a Full- or Half-Day Meeting of the Council

Depending on the agenda, schedule the amount of time needed for the meeting. Of course, you'll want to be considerate of participants' schedules and the availability of meeting facilities.

5. Establish an Agenda and Hold a Council Meeting

Make this one of the most interesting and engaging meetings anyone has ever attended. Budget the time as carefully as you would if you were budgeting finances. Consider each program element as an investment of time, talent, energy, knowledge, and experience that pays off in good thinking and the generation of ideas.

Let's assume that the primary purpose of the council meeting is to identify "the characteristics of an education system capable of preparing students for life in a global knowledge/information age." What might specifically be included in the meeting agenda? The following is a list of likely components (see Appendix D for a detailed sample agenda):

- A briefing on local, national, and international issues and trends
- An explanation of the specific process to be used
- Participation in small groups to identify characteristics of an education system capable of preparing students for life in a global knowledge/information age
- Continuation of small-group work, with placement of characteristics into categories and development of summary statements
- Reporting the work of each small group to the entire council and considering similarities and differences among categories
- Closing remarks to express thanks and share next steps

6. Do the Follow-Up: Expand Involvement and Prepare and Release Results

To broaden your base, to test the characteristics identified by the council, and to tap the thinking of an expanded group of people, you will likely want to take the following steps.

First, you should edit the characteristics for clarity and format but not to change their intent. Then you might expand this diverse group of council members by an additional 40 to 50 advisors. Using a modified Delphi process (as described in Chapter 6), you can develop and then distribute a questionnaire by regular mail or e-mail. In that questionnaire, ask members of this expanded group to select from the council's list what they consider the 12, 20, or some other number of items they believe will be most important in preparing students for life in a global knowledge/information age. You might also ask them to list items that they believe should have been included but were not.

In a second-round questionnaire to the same group, list the characteristics in rank order, depending on the number of selections the items received in round one. Ask participants to suggest any re-ranking and to judge each characteristic based on its potential impact on the ability to prepare students for the future—high, medium, or low. Also request that they speculate on when the characteristic might become commonplace, ranging from "It's happening now" to "It will never happen," with other choices on a scale that includes options for the short term, medium term, and long term.

When the results of round two are complete and tabulated, develop one or more one-sentence statements to encompass each cluster of characteristics. In a report, each cluster will be followed by some combination of the supporting items. The reason for this telescoping is not to change intent but to make the items more understandable, less repetitive, and easier to communicate. Figure 7.1 is an example of statements that capture the work of one particular council that sought to define how schools and school systems might be shaped as they prepare students for life in a global knowledge/information age.

Finally, you'll want to prepare and release a final report and put the information to use in developing your vision. In addition to clarifying the vision you want to pursue, this process will also affect the planning of the organization, stimulate discussion, set future agendas, demonstrate the wisdom of the staff and community, and build both ownership and esprit de corps.

7.1	16 Characteristics of Schools and School Systems for the 21st Century

1. The definitions of "school," "teacher," and "learner" are reshaped by the digital world.
2. All students have an equal opportunity for an outstanding education, with adequate funding, no matter where they live.
3. Educators are driven by high expectations and clear, challenging standards that are widely understood by students, families, and communities.
4. A project-based "curriculum for life" engages students in addressing real-world problems, issues important to humanity, and questions that matter.
5. Teachers and administrators are effectively prepared for the global knowledge/information age.
6. Students, schools, school systems, and communities are connected around the clock with each other and with the world through information-rich, interactive technology.
7. School systems conduct, consider, and apply significant research in designing programs that lead to constantly improving student achievement.
8. Students learn to think, reason, make sound decisions, and demonstrate values inherent in a democracy.
9. School facilities provide a safe, secure, stimulating, and joyous learning environment that contributes to a lifelong passion for learning and high student achievement.
10. Leadership is collaborative, and governance is focused on broad issues that affect student learning.
11. Students learn about other cultures, respect and honor diversity, and see the world as an extended neighborhood.
12. Schools promote creativity and teamwork at all levels, and teachers help students turn information into knowledge and knowledge into wisdom.
13. Assessment of student progress is performance-based, taking into account students' individual talents, abilities, and aspirations.
14. A student-centered, collaboratively developed vision provides power and focus for education community-wide.
15. Continuous improvement is a driving force in every school and school system.
16. Schools are the crossroads and central convening point of the community.

Source: From *Preparing Schools and School Systems for the 21st Century* (pp. 4–5), by Frank Withrow with Harvey Long and Gary Marx, 1999, Arlington, VA: American Association of School Administrators.

Results of the visioning process might be shared more broadly through news releases, a news conference, a Web cast, cable or broadcast television, radio programs, and newsletters. Consider setting aside agenda time at meetings of boards, parents, faculty and staff, students, service clubs, and other types of community groups.

Use the results not as the final word, but as a means for stirring ongoing discussion about the future you would like to see for the education system and its students. Some of those discussions are sure to energize people to focus on what is important, such as the implications of these characteristics for what educators do, how they do it, and what students need to know and be able to do.

Identifying Characteristics: Examples from Real Life

The sections that follow provide examples of actual processes used in three different situations. The first describes a process used at the national level to identify characteristics of the schools and school systems we need for the future. The second describes a process used by a local school system and community to enhance their strategic planning. And the third describes a process used to help identify the future characteristics of a country.

A National Effort on the Future of Education

During 1998–99, serving as a senior executive and later as a consultant for the American Association of School Administrators, I initiated a project that led to a publication titled *Preparing Schools and School Systems for the 21st Century* (Withrow et al., 1999). A distinguished Council of 21, composed of leaders in education, business, government, and other fields, met at a conference at Mount Vernon in Virginia under the honorary chairmanship of gravity-breaking astronaut and former U.S. senator John Glenn.

The group identified more than 250 characteristics of schools and school systems capable of preparing students for life in a global knowledge/

information age. As a follow-up activity, a two-round modified Delphi process helped to sort, clarify, and expand on each of those items. Finally, a list of 16 major characteristics was developed (see Figure 7.1). That list of 16 embodied the intent of the 250 characteristics but was clearer, less voluminous, and more easily communicated. Each of the 16 characteristics was reinforced by specific, more discrete characteristics identified during this rigorous process.

Results were published in book form and distributed nationwide. A news conference announcing the results was carried on the Internet. The purpose was not to suggest that these characteristics should describe every education system. Instead, the aim was to capture the interest of education systems and to urge them to undertake a similar process in their own communities.

A Local Effort to Enhance Strategic Planning

The Orange North Supervisory Union, a school district in Williamstown, Vermont, used a version of this identification process to enhance its strategic planning. Superintendent Douglas Shiok, working with the Williamstown School Board and Select Board, appointed a Williamstown Future Trends Council. The 21 members of the council met in the Senate chamber of the Vermont State House in Montpelier. The six-and-a-half-hour meeting began with introductions and the presentation of a report containing demographic and other data, followed by a presentation on 10 trends affecting society. The council members were then divided into five small groups that were asked to identify what schools were doing well in dealing with each trend, and what schools could or should be doing to deal with each of those trends. Each small group reported to the entire council on what it had identified. Following these reports, participants formed two small groups whose task was to identify implications of the trends for the entire community, not just the schools. The two groups reported on their findings, and based on these discussions, the council was asked to provide advice for the leadership team. The meeting concluded with a closing statement from the superintendent, who thanked the participants and explained how the wisdom shared at the meeting would be considered in strategic planning.

According to a local newspaper that covered the historic event, some of the ideas or possible characteristics discussed by the council included the following:

- A possible virtual school
- Financial flexibility to help attract and retain quality teachers
- Bridging a perceived communications gap
- The need to have a broad range of educational alternatives
- A commitment to pursuing what is best for students in preparing them for a fast-changing world
- Getting beyond the status quo
- The need to pursue the future while considering what the community can and is willing to afford

In his concluding remarks to the group, Superintendent Shiok said, "I have learned more about Williamstown today in six hours than I have in the last five years. We need to be thinking about education in an entirely different way" (Delcore, 2002, pp. 1, 8).

Identifying Characteristics of a Country

A process for identifying the desirable characteristics of an organization can also be applied to developing a vision of a state, a province, a country, or even the world. I have worked with thoughtful citizens of many countries to help them understand broad societal trends and, in certain cases, to help them describe the nation they want to become.

In one country, I asked diverse groups of people in the national capital and several provinces to identify the characteristics of the country they would like to see in their bicentennial year, 2010. This country has suffered through authoritarian regimes and severe economic setbacks.

Meetings took place in cities, towns, and villages. The gatherings were held at schools, universities, city halls, newspaper offices, foundation headquarters, hotels, government facilities, nongovernmental organization offices, private homes, and in numerous other settings. The sessions generally involved people ranging from high school students to older citizens, as well as leaders in business, education, government, and other fields.

After one of those meetings, a participant distilled the characteristics that were identified into a vision for his country. The following is a slightly edited version of his vision statement that does not reveal his country or his full name for reasons of privacy:

> In 2010, I will be 56 years old. Susy will be 60, Pablo 24, and Natalia 21. I want for them a country where anyone would like to live.
>
> - A country where children are taken care of, old people are respected, and opportunities are plentiful for all the rest.
> - A country where optimism enlightens our future.
> - A country where honest and capable people achieve success based on their merits.
> - A country where solidarity is based on justice, not charity.
> - A country that takes advantage of its human and natural resources and leaves to our children a larger heritage than the one we received.
> - A nation that is proud of its involvement in the global world and contributes in a balanced and just way to universal causes.
> - A society where children are born with smiles on their faces and have more reasons to smile as they grow and develop.
> - A country that can say it has finally emerged and will continue to emerge each minute in the future.
> - A country of 40 million people, celebrating after years of hard work and melded into a large world embrace.

Reputations and Legacies

How do you want to be seen or remembered—both in terms of your organization and as an individual? The process for identifying characteristics of the organization of the future can also help in considering the reputation you'd like to develop. Ask three key questions to guide the process:

1. How would people currently describe your school, school system, college/university, or other organization, and how would they describe you as an individual?
2. How would you like them to describe you and your organization by [year]?
3. Considering the discrepancy, how will you get from where you are to where you want to be?

The same steps that help build better organizations can help improve personal reputations or build the legacies that are left for families, communities, and future generations.

Questions and Activities

1. Engage a group of people, with representatives from both internal and external publics, in responding to a question such as: What are the characteristics of an education system capable of preparing students for life in a global knowledge/information age? (Form an appropriate question for your particular institution or profession.)
2. Conceive of a process for your organization similar to the one suggested in this chapter. Develop a name for your council, draft an agenda, consider a meeting venue, and develop a post-meeting agenda for making the findings of the council a part of ongoing planning and action.
3. Either in a group or by regular mail or e-mail, ask people how they believe people on the street would describe your organization today. Then ask how they would like the organization to be described. Consider the discrepancy and what might have to happen to move from the reputation you have to the reputation you would like to have.

Readings

Withrow, F. (with Long, H., & Marx, G.). (1999). *Preparing schools and school systems for the 21st century*. Arlington, VA: American Association of School Administrators.

8 Scenarios: "What If?" and "Then What?"

We're talking about changes in basic assumptions ... few traditional organizations ever go through the eye of the needle.

—Peter Senge (2002)

People have been asking "what if" and "then what" questions for centuries. For anyone thinking about the future, there are benefits to developing and playing out these types of scenarios. They can, in fact, help us describe, discuss, debate, and decide on the directions we want to go and the actions we want to take (Chase, 1984).

It's almost like a game. We've scanned our internal and external environments, perhaps involving dozens or hundreds of people in the process. We've studied the macroenvironment, looking closely at political, economic, social, technological, environmental, demographic, and educational trends and thought about their possible implications. We've considered our values and the values of those we serve or depend on for our success. We've identified issues and sorted them to determine which have a high probability of affecting our organization and its objectives. Our next step might be to frame our assumptions and develop our scenarios.

What Is a Scenario?

How often has someone asked, "OK, so what's the scenario?" In response, we very likely described a future course of events—what we hoped might happen. The term itself grew from the theater, where it generally referred to a sketch or vignette. Michel Godet (2001), a noted strategist and professor at Cnam (National Conservatory for Arts and Industries) in Paris, calls scenarios "coherent sets of hypotheses leading from a given original situation to a future situation" (p. 18).

RAND Europe (n.d.) describes a scenario as "a coherent picture of a plausible future." The key word here is "plausible." Don't immediately reject far-out possibilities, those that might seem overly creative or even outrageous. First ask, "What are the circumstances that could cause this to happen?" If you can't identify any, the assumption or scenario might not be plausible. On the other hand, it could show up as a wildcard or as an unintended consequence of some seemingly unrelated future decision. It could be beyond imagination.

Those who have worked with RAND generally consider the organization a pioneer in the use of scenarios as a policy analysis tool. RAND's snapshots of the future are used "to deal with the uncertainty about what the future could bring" (RAND Europe, n.d.). They are not forecasts or predictions, just descriptions of alternative futures.

The World Future Society, in a special report called "The Art of Foresight," refers to scenarios as "attempts to imagine future possibilities on the basis of what we know (or think we know). Scenarios are useful in helping us understand what might happen as a result of a decision we may make" (2004, p. 4).

As connected leaders, in our constant quest for coherence, we are expected to consider how we will read and project our environment, organize our thinking, and develop our assumptions. That process is often called *system analysis*. Following a path similar to the one outlined in this book, we can conceive of a *preferred future*, an *unpreferred future*, or just a *possible future*. Scenarios are, in essence, alternative futures.

In analyzing any possible scenario, the conversation generally turns to these questions: What possible side effects could develop? What about unintended consequences? Ignoring these questions opens the door to being blindsided. Of course, some things may be beyond our imaginations. They come at us out of the blue. They are called *wildcards*, and they can operate either to our advantage or disadvantage.

What Are the Steps in Developing Scenarios?

This book has been devoted, in large part, to steps that precede the actual development of scenarios, such as understanding the environment. For the sake of coherence, let's review a few of the first rungs on the ladder. Then we'll climb to the top.

1. Analyze the Environment

It's important to scan the environment continually, because the world is changing at warp speed. We can use the processes described in Chapters 4, 5, and 6, such as trends analysis, PEST, SWOT, or others, to better understand the possible implications of societal forces for our school, school system, college, university, or other organization. Scanning can provide an early warning system and suggest what trends, issues, or other forces require close monitoring.

While we're examining issues that specifically affect our organization, we should also put on our generalist's hat. We should consider broad trends and issues that affect not only our immediate environment, but also our industry and the whole of society. Those mega-issues that seemed of little consequence yesterday, for example, could lead to a softer economy, lower valuations of property, less tax revenue or spendable income, and tighter budgets. Trends and issues at any level may eventually roll over us unless we're ready for them.

2. Monitor Changes in the Environment

James Morrison and Ian Wilson (1997), in an article titled "Analyzing Environments and Developing Scenarios in Uncertain Times," suggest that once trends and potential issues or events are identified, a conscious effort should be launched to monitor them. The "issue brief" model illustrated in Chapter 5 could provide a format for keeping information, events, and possibilities fresh.

3. List Factors Essential to Success

Which factors do we believe to be important to our success, as we can see or anticipate from our current vantage point? Money? The ability to attract and keep talented people? Social and economic conditions? Property values and assessed valuations? Federal and state laws or other interventions? The aging or maturity level of the community? Internal and external expectations? The ability to acquire and effectively use technology? The ability to earn and maintain community support? Flexibility to respond to a fast-changing environment?

This list is by no means complete. It is presented only to spark further thinking about factors that affect our chances to provide sound education and generally become even more effective in our chosen mission. A further question might be, "What assumptions did you make in proposing the factor you've just mentioned?" We will likely want to develop three or four credible assumptions about each factor to spur discussion, debate, and decision.

To further understand this step, let's look beyond factors that generally serve as a foundation for good education. For example, suppose we were considering our energy future. Imagine that we're charged with developing scenarios addressing future energy consumption and the fuels we might need. In that case, the factors we identify would likely include availability of current sources of energy, price fluctuations, clean air laws and regulations that would lead to "decarbonizing," international protocols, the rate of development and adoption of new energy-producing technologies, the decommissioning of some types of power plants, and the likelihood that people will be willing to conserve energy.

4. Put the Scenario Development Process in Perspective

The future is, by nature, increasingly unpredictable as we extend it beyond a certain length of time and patterns of predictable behavior. For example, whether our planet remains habitable depends not only on our stewardship today, but also on the tender loving care of future generations. Although that future behavior isn't necessarily predictable, it could be influenced by education.

Nonetheless, some things are predictable. That's why scenarios take on added value. They can help "steer us on a middle course between a misguided reliance on prediction and a despairing belief that we can do nothing but envision the future and therefore cannot shape it," according to Morrison and Wilson (1997). They describe scenarios as "stories of possible futures that the institution might encounter."

5. Consider Assumptions

We've asked, "What factors are essential to our success?" We've identified some of the assumptions that support each of those factors. Now it's time to test our assumptions.

Figure 8.1 provides a glimpse of three assumptions, all focused on the aging of a community and the resulting impact on school enrollment. As we study these assumptions, we might ask, "What is the level of certainty that this statement will describe our future?" The range might run from "a high level of certainty" to "highly unlikely." Then we might ask, "What impact will this assumption have on our education system's ability to reach its goals?" The choices are high, medium, or low impact. If an assumption is high in certainty and high in impact, it will likely find a place in our scenario(s). This approach is a hybrid of the Probability/Impact Matrix, described in Chapter 5. The bottom line is this: our assumptions will play a significant role in helping us build our scenarios.

6. Develop Scenarios That Represent Alternative Futures

Based on our scanning, monitoring, and consideration of basic assumptions, we're ready to take the next step—the actual development of three or four scenarios. Each will be one to two pages in length.

John Ratcliffe, director of the Faculty of the Environment at the Dublin Institute of Technology in Ireland, suggests we construct something

8.1	A Sample Matrix for Testing Assumptions		
Question What impact will aging have on enrollment during the next five years?			
Assumption	**Level of Certainty** (Circle one)	**Impact** (Circle one)	
The aging of our community will continue, resulting in more empty-nesters and fewer homes with school-age children, leading to an average enrollment decline of 2 percent during each of the next five years.	H M L	H M L	
Older residents of the community will move to retirement communities at the rate of 2 percent a year and sell their homes to younger families, leading to an average enrollment increase of 1 percent during each of the next five years.	H M L	H M L	
Developers are likely to purchase blocks of homes vacated by older citizens. Those neighborhoods will then be converted to high-density housing, leading to enrollment increases of 2 percent a year.	H M L	H M L	
Note: H = High, M = Medium, L = Low.			

resembling "a set of stories built around carefully constructed plots." Each represents "a plausible alternative future against which policy options can be tested and implications identified," he adds (Ratcliffe, 2003).

The scenarios themselves offer distinct choices, highlighting alternative images generated through our discussions of trends and issues. Each presents quantitative data as well as qualitative perspectives related to the key factors we identified earlier. Generally, each scenario is given a distinct title to reflect its "uniquenesses" and "discontinuities" with others.

Often, a fascinating phenomenon occurs. When seeing a scenario as a "whole cloth" and comparing it to others, someone is likely to express surprise. First, the jaw drops and the eyes open wide. Then, this advocate for "the one and only way" finds himself questioning previous assumptions.

Writing for *Futures Research Quarterly*, Ratcliffe (2003) notes that scenarios can help "create a learning organization possessing a common vocabulary and an effective basis for communicating complex—sometimes paradoxical—conditions and options." He describes good scenarios as both "plausible and surprising. They have the power to break old stereotypes. And, by rehearsing tomorrow's future, they produce better decisions today" (pp. 7–8).

To illustrate, let's consider three scenarios an imaginary school system might develop as it looks five years into the future. The scenarios are based on current and historic data on enrollment, demographics, race/ethnicity of students, economics and mobility of the community, percentage of families with school-age children, summary results of educational program assessments, and funding. (See Appendix E for expanded versions of the three scenarios, including additional background information.)

In this imaginary district, Acme City Unified School District #88, enrollment has been increasing slightly, after several years of decline; the student body is increasingly diverse, with a growing percentage of immigrant children who speak a variety of languages. The departure of several local businesses has recently been counteracted by the arrival of a high-tech firm. Although many high- and middle-income families have left the district over the past 10 years, others are beginning to move into the area. The academic performance of the district's students is showing signs of improvement, though achievement is generally below state averages. A state law limits increases in annual school budgets, but an override provision allows for modest increases with voters' approval. The district's operating budget is increasingly reliant on state revenues, but a statewide economic downturn has reduced those revenues. Because its costs are rising faster than revenues, the district has had to cut back on staff and programs.

Scenario 1: A Glimmer at the End of the Tunnel. *Assumptions:* Enrollments increase slightly. The racial/ethnic makeup of the district stabilizes. A tax override passes. Student achievement is up slightly. First- and second-generation immigrants climb the economic ladder and remain in the community, while gentrification brings some middle- and high-income people back into older parts of the city.

Scenario 2: The Headlamp of an Oncoming Train. *Assumptions:* A tax override is defeated. A souring state economy leads to drastic cuts in financial support. Immigrant populations increase substantially, requiring additional programs. Enrollments decline. Businesses and middle- to high-income families continue to move out of the city. Demand intensifies for the district to meet state and federal standards.

Scenario 3: Sunlight at the End of the Tunnel. *Assumptions:* A tax override passes, opening the door to substantial increases in the budget. The state economy improves, resulting in even greater levels of state support. First- and second-generation immigrants are intent on pursuing education, becoming entrepreneurs, and building the local economy. New businesses and hundreds of new jobs are created. Student achievement goes up. The community develops a winning attitude about its future.

7. Consider the Scenarios That Have Been Developed

How should we consider these scenarios? Methodology is important. For example, as we did with our preliminary assumptions, we might ask the scenario team and perhaps other groups, large and small, to judge each scenario based on its likelihood and potential impact.

In discussing each of the scenarios, we will likely pose questions such as these: Which represents the most likely future? Which represents the worst possible scenario? Which represents our preferred future, or the best possible scenario?

Whole scenarios, or parts of them, might be considered desirable or undesirable. In fact, the process could actually lead us to the development of an alternative, something we might call a *meta-scenario*. In considering how to compose any type or level of scenario, a RAND team concluded that each must be brief and useful "for policy making in a practical sense." It must also "cover a sufficiently broad range of possible futures to provide a robust basis for informing policy decisions" (Silberglitt & Hove, n.d., pp. 304–305).

8. Use What You've Learned in Developing Plans

The process used in developing and considering scenarios reveals information and directions that can have significant value for planning and decision making. Recommendations from the scenario team might apply to long-term, short-term, or immediate plans and decisions.

9. Take Needed Action

With informed plans and decisions in place based on this extensive but exciting approach to creating a future, we're on our way to working side-by-side with colleagues to take needed action. It's time to move our strategies forward—to take action. To assist us, RAND (n.d.) describes "*hedging strategies* to help ensure that we can cope with *undesirable* futures (or take advantage of desirable ones) and *shaping strategies* to help ensure we can achieve *desirable* futures."

10. Monitor Progress and Continue the Cycle

As noted many times, the world is moving very quickly. The status quo is nothing more than a ticket to obsolescence. Only decades ago, organizations were able to establish and freeze policies and programs, and with minor adjustments, pursue them for years. Today, in a world of exponential change, creating a future must be a continuous, never-ending process. Our strategies should be alive and flexible, not buried or embedded on the top shelf. Scanning and planning should be continuous. The process should never stop.

Who Should Be Involved in the Scenario Process?

We've already involved numerous people, representing staff and the community, in the ongoing process of scanning the environment. Now we're faced with using what we've learned to enhance our planning and decision making. As this chapter makes clear, scenarios seem to be a next logical step, but who should be involved in the process?

Frequently, a scenario team is appointed to lead the way. Team members are the people who will oversee, craft, and test scenarios. However, their first job is to be sure they have the support and involvement of management. Otherwise, the whole process could turn out to be nothing more than a highly interesting exercise.

The team itself will likely include representatives of various groups or departments within the organization and perhaps segments of the community. Making sure diverse interests are included will enrich the process and the mix of scenarios. Subgroups might be appointed to investigate and develop assumptions around various factors important to education, or any other field or industry. At certain points, the scenario team might hold sessions that attract many more members of the staff and community. Questionnaires might be distributed by regular mail or e-mail. An astute facilitator should orchestrate idea generation for each meeting or process.

Thinking might be enriched by the testimony of futurists, management consultants, scientists, demographers, economists, technologists, politicians, journalists, and perhaps others. Occasionally, a maverick thinker might be brought in to stir outside-the-box thinking.

A champion should be appointed to lead the scenario team. Ideally, the leader should be widely respected, approachable but above reproach, an advocate for the process but not a cheerleader for one position over another, and a stimulating presence who can encourage the best thinking from all who are involved (Ratcliffe, 2003).

Scenario Logistics

In developing scenarios, those involved will ask some obvious and some not-so-obvious questions. Each deserves attention. Here are a few that are likely to arise.

What are the characteristics of a sound scenario? Morrison and Wilson (1997) suggest that scenarios should be plausible, be structurally different, be internally consistent, reflect decision making utility, and challenge the organization's conventional wisdom about the future. They should be different enough from each other that they offer distinct choices. Another important point: In each case, we should be able to say, "This scenario could actually happen, whatever decision we make about its likelihood."

How many scenarios should we develop? Use good sense. Obviously, we could find endless combinations of societal and other forces and formulate dozens of possibilities. However, the number should be kept to three or four at the most. Peter Schwartz (1995) recommends against three, because "people are tempted to identify one of them as the middle or most likely."

A RAND (n.d.) analysis focused on a number of scenarios exploring energy futures. Two are highlighted here:

- The World Energy Council and the International Institute for Applied Systems Analysis analyzed six possible futures related to energy that fell within three broad categories. Each of those scenarios spanned the globe and extended to the year 2100; they demonstrated the dependence of energy futures on geopolitics, policy intervention, and the world economy.
- Royal Dutch Shell, a pioneer in this type of analysis, displayed two distinct scenarios. One was "sustained growth," based on a business-as-usual strategy. Another was a "dematerialization" scenario, which looked at possible rapid changes in consumer lifestyles and technologies that could reduce the absolute world demand for energy. For example, rather than continuing to rely heavily on petroleum products, the world might dramatically increase its use of renewable sources of energy.

Is it possible to develop scenarios for each factor, such as technology, finance, or community support? Yes. The process would likely resemble the one used to test basic assumptions. Eventually, the pieces need to come together in a set of scenarios that span the entire organization. We all know that what affects one part of the organization will likely affect other parts as well.

Models, Pilot Tests, and Simulations: The Offspring of Scenarios

By examining what is happening in the real world, we can sometimes create a model to clearly translate what we are sensing into something concrete. If two or more models exist, they can be pitted against each other to generate discussion and debate. In fact, we might even hold brainstorming sessions to speculate on how each of the models could be improved.

Taking the process a step further, we could decide to set up one or more pilot programs and compare results over time. Of course, this is not a new concept. These types of "try-outs" have been going on for years, providing an opportunity to compare a control group with a variety of other methods for reaching a goal. After trying a certain approach with a smaller group, we might decide to take it systemwide.

Sophisticated computer simulations can also create an opportunity to mathematically determine certain scenarios' impact on the bottom line—on a budget, for example. These sophisticated systems, in common use, allow fairly quick answers to "what if" questions, according to the World Future Society (2004).

Caution: Beware of Rocks on the Road to the Future

It's sunny, and you're driving down the road without a care in the world. Your favorite CD is filling the car with sweet music. The cruise control is set, and you're doing a steady 60 miles per hour. At this rate, you'll be at your meeting by 4 p.m.

First you see the sign: "Road Work Ahead." Then you see the equipment, the rocks in the road, and another sign that reads "Detour Next Five Miles." The detour crosses a railroad track, but not for a while, because an 82-car train is parked on the crossing. What seemed simple has now become more complex.

As we sail along toward the future, we need to be certain that we are ready for the rocks in the road. We also need to guard against creating our own rocks that could block our path or weigh us down. Here are a few typical cautions for anyone considering scenarios for the future.

Are we asking the right questions? Sometimes we come up with astute answers to questions that don't matter that much.

Are there forces that keep us from asking the right questions? A bias for the status quo can throw up a roadblock that keeps us from thoroughly considering assumptions and possible scenarios. Some issues may simply never be mentioned. They have become "the elephant in the room," invisible deterrents that keep certain critical discussions off the agenda. Conformity to one point of view can stifle the very ideas and forces that could help an organization achieve a successful and legitimate future.

Is the process sophisticated enough to deal with the complexity of the issue? This question spins off a couple of others: How often do we complain about people who seem to always have simple solutions to complicated problems? Does our system or our culture allow us to dig deeply into a vast array of trends or sensitive and complex issues? In a fast-changing world, getting everyone involved in a legitimate process of creating a future can keep the organization on the cutting edge and make life a lot more interesting.

Have we considered the possibility of error? Canadian futurist Kimon Valaskakis suggests a medical analogy when considering whether we're on the right track (Godet, 2001). For example, a physician might take the wrong turn in diagnosing a disease, in forecasting its development, in prescribing the right drugs, and in determining the right dosage. Although each is important, the first step can cause a cascade that involves all the rest. Think about how the analogy can be applied in an education setting.

Do facts have a chance in the face of myth? "We have a tradition of excellence. The money we've needed has always been there. Nothing can stop us now." Perhaps no other premise is so dangerous to organizational health as the assumption that the goose will continue to lay the golden egg. Believing can be a step in making it so, but if the myth is based solely on historic inertia, beware. The world is very likely moving faster than you are.

What are our attitudes about the future? Is the prospect of creating a future a threat, or does it get the juices flowing? Is the very thought of it interesting and exciting? French futurist Michel Godet suggests that people generally demonstrate five attitudes about the future (2001, p. 18):

- Passive—the ostrich accepting change as it comes
- Reactive—the firefighter waiting for the alarm to ring
- Preactive—the insurance agent preparing for foreseeable change, believing that an ounce of prevention is worth a pound of cure
- Proactive—the provocateur who pushes for desirable change
- A combination of reactive, preactive, and proactive

An Example from History

To close this chapter, let's consider some scenarios with a historical slant. Let's put ourselves in the position of King Ferdinand and Queen Isabella of Spain. It's the late 15th century, and we've asked a commission to make a recommendation on whether we should support a voyage to find a western passage to the Indies. The commission is headed by Hernando de Talavera, archbishop of Granada. Christopher Columbus is nudging us for a decision, telling us that there's only water between Spain and the coast of China, which he has said over and over again is a mere 3,500 miles away. Talavera suggests six reasons why we should scrap the idea (Godet, 2001, p. 21):

1. A journey to Asia will take at least three years.
2. The ocean is infinite and perhaps unnavigable.
3. If Columbus should reach the ends of the earth, he would not be able to return.
4. There are no endpoints of land, because most of the globe is covered with water. Saint Augustine said so.
5. Of the five parts of the world, only three are inhabitable.
6. So many centuries after the Creation, it is unlikely that lands of any interest could remain undiscovered.

Faced with this conflicting advice, the king and queen still wanted to support Columbus. They very likely considered at least three scenarios as they pondered the possible outcomes of their patronage:

- **Scenario 1:** Columbus will discover a new trade route to China. He will return in triumph, and the king and queen will be revered for their foresight. Their country will become powerful and wealthy, and the monarchs will end up even more rich and famous.
- **Scenario 2:** After three years, Columbus will return, having found nothing but more water. Never striking land beyond his stopover at the Canary Islands off the coast of Africa, he comes back empty-handed. The king and queen are ridiculed for "wasting" scarce resources on folly and accused of harboring visions of grandeur.
- **Scenario 3:** Columbus never returns. Along with his ships and crew, he is presumed to have fallen off the edge of the earth. Columbus is declared a hero for his great courage, and the king and queen are blamed for his death. The people demand that they be deposed.

For better or worse, the king and queen decided to put their money on something like Scenario 1. However, what really happened was a wildcard, something they didn't expect. A huge landmass, later called America, lay in the ocean between Europe and Asia. As for Columbus, he reached America and didn't fully realize it. The rest, as they say, is history.

Questions and Activities

1. After considering political, economic, social, technological, environmental, demographic, and other issues and trends, develop three reasonable but different scenarios for the future of your organization, profession, or industry.
2. Consider the nature of the organization that will be most viable in the next two years. Plan back from your best possible scenario to the actions you might need to take to get you there.
3. Identify the types of people who should be involved in a scenario team for your organization. Why would you consider selecting them?

4. Conceive of a scenario process that helps your organization develop and select from alternative futures. Draw from this chapter as you consider the steps you will take.

Readings

Godet, M. (2001). *Creating futures: Scenario planning as a management tool.* London: Economica Ltd.

Morrison, J. L., & Wilson, I. (1997). Analyzing environments and developing scenarios in uncertain times. In M. W. Peterson, D. D. Dill, L. A. Mets, & Associates (Eds.), *Planning and management for a changing environment.* San Francisco: Jossey-Bass. Available: http://www.horizon.unc.edu/courses/papers/JBChapter.asp

Ratcliffe, J. (2003, Winter). Scenario planning: An evaluation of practice. *Futures Research Quarterly, (19)*4, 5–25.

PART 4

Future-Focused Communication

To a great extent, this entire book is about strategic, future-focused communication. Everything, after all, starts with relationships, whether those relationships are among people or ideas.

We've discussed the need for leaders to be connected not only to those they serve but also to those they depend on to provide services or lend their support. We've explored some techniques for scanning our internal and external environments and for conceiving of a vision for the future. Now it's time to put strategic, future-focused communication into context and to share some added ideas for getting people connected to the future we hope to create.

9 | Strategic Communication

Spin doctors can remedy an ailment, but rarely can they cure the disease.

—Sam Singer (1995)

For too long, for too many organizations, a good defense has been their primary offense. Success was a matter of fending off change. The typical mindset could be characterized like this: *"Questions? Suggestions? Recommendations? Concerns? They sound like attacks to me. First, let's prove that we've been right all along. Then, let's discredit the people who made those scurrilous attacks. Who knows what impact this could have on our policies, our programs, our bottom line, and our ideology! Report to your battle stations!"* Today, in a world of exploding diversity and exponential change, any organization with this attitude might wake up to find that it has successfully isolated itself from society, with little understanding of what its valuable role might be.

The *status quo* is formally defined as "the existing state of affairs." Another definition could be "a ticket to obsolescence." Let's face it—there is no more "business as usual." There is no more status quo. We're headed one way or the other, either toward breakthroughs or breakdowns.

Jaap van Ginneken, who is affiliated with the Amsterdam School of Communications, puts it this way: "All too often, we approach opinions and attitudes as if they were a brick with an obvious permanence." In addition to examining issues microscopically, he says, we need to look at them "macroscopically," in a broader social context (Adams, 2003).

Strategic Communication: The Key to a Living Strategy

We've worked through the process of scanning the environment and developed a vision for the future. We have a plan. That plan has been informed and energized by engaging people and listening to their ideas. Building sound relationships and staying in touch will help turn the plan into a living strategy.

Strategic, future-focused communication and leadership are inextricably linked. In a world that is changing rapidly, we are constantly challenged to bring coherence to information, ideas, and events that might otherwise be seen as unfamiliar, even chaotic.

Sure, we need to pay attention to daily and hourly needs. Not everything is about "the future." There *is* a "here and now." However, we need to get past the tops of our desks and broaden our frame to make sure we are considering the needs and culture of our community and the whole of society. What we do or do not do today, what we say or do not say, and how it is perceived in the broader community, could have a profound impact on our short-term and long-term success.

In a complex, often unpredictable environment, much of what we do might seem random as we address needs and opportunities that flash before us. That's all the more reason our communication must be strategic and connected to our aspirations for the future. Put another way, it means that dealing with the issues of the day is important but can't be substituted for a coherent approach to addressing the needs of a fast-moving, ever-changing environment.

There are few, if any, one-shot deals in communication. That's another reason why our communication should be, to the extent possible, future-focused and strategic. We need to be sure that as many bases as possible are covered, and that we're also prepared for those things that come at us out of the blue.

As leaders, it's up to us to inform the process—to arrange for the people who will do the research, explore financial needs, make the presentations, listen, and respond to questionnaires that help us stay close to those we serve. It's our responsibility to ensure that the system is open to new ideas, that it welcomes ingenuity, and that it is limber enough to bend with the sway of a society that is constantly in motion.

Leadership expert Warren Bennis (2002) has noted how the changing nature of communication technology has changed the nature of the work-place. Compared with earlier generations, we have an enormous amount of information at our fingertips, and we can communicate it more quickly than ever before. To top it all off, the technology is interactive. "We're going to be able to talk simultaneously to a lot more people than we ever thought possible," says Bennis. "That means we're going to have to democratize the workplace even more" (p. 157).

Communication: A Definition and Guidelines

What is communication? A key to understanding? A connection? A bridge? The weave in the fabric of society? An essential part of leadership and management? Pick one, or feel free to select "all of the above." One thing is certain: Communication is our only route, perhaps our only hope, for helping people discover a common purpose, determine the common good, establish a sense of community, and develop a commitment to pursuing a common future.

In this chapter, we could discuss any number of key communication functions, such as how to give a good speech or write a news release. We could examine the thought process that goes into composing a message or the best ways to conduct a formal or informal opinion poll. We could zero in on interpersonal communication and make a justified case that listening skills, nonverbal communication, and excising fear from an organization are crucial to ultimate success.

Instead, we'll assume some knowledge about the basics and suggest a few ways that we can make communication even more future-focused and strategic. That kind of communication assumes the following:

- A leadership commitment to encouraging generative thinking among staff and the community to support a true learning organization
- A commitment to constantly scanning the environment and listening to our publics
- An understanding of the need to frequently redefine the identity of the organization or community as it changes
- A dedication to an ongoing process of developing and renewing a strategic vision
- An understanding that communication, to be effective, needs to be pervasive, a part of everything we do

Organized communication should help to develop relationships among both people and ideas. It should include both internal and external publics. Communicating should never be seen as a one-shot deal. It is continuous and should never stop. Let's expand on a few of these concepts.

Get connected to the world of ideas. Unfortunately, when we think of communication in an organization, we too often consider it to be only writing, speaking, and working with the news media. All are important. However, strategic, future-focused communication requires us to make even more intense use of our critical and creative thinking skills. Our aim is to be constantly connected with the internal and external environments and to consider how to make sense of the complexity and chaos that have become an ongoing part of a fast-moving society. Building relationships among people is essential. So is building relationships among ideas.

Involve internal and external publics. Traditionally, planning for communication starts with identifying key internal and external publics, determining what they need to know, and then deciding how we'll listen to, inform, or involve them. Frequently, organizations will involve an entire school staff in the process of responding to these types of questions and actually developing a plan. Internal publics, people such as teachers, have a direct relationship with the education system. External publics, such as parents, taxpayers who are not parents, and public officials, might have an indirect relationship. Figure 9.1 presents key questions that will lead to a basic two-way communication plan based both on informing others and informing ourselves.

9.1	Developing a Basic Communication Plan	
Steps	**Questions to Ask**	
	Informing Others	Informing Ourselves
1. Identify publics.	Who needs to know or understand?	• Whose advice or support do we need? • Who will be affected by our decisions?
2. Determine content.	• What do these publics need to know or under-stand? • What do they want to know?	• What do we want to know or under-stand? • What do people know and not know? • What do people understand or mis-understand? • How strongly do people feel about an issue?
3. Decide how to make contact.	How should we inform or involve these publics?	How should we listen to these publics?

Be sure communication is ongoing. To be effective, communication must be ongoing, a continuous process reinforced by a panoply of vehicles, processes, and programs. These generally include newsletters; Web sites (both Internet and intranet); advisory committees; annual, accountability, and other reports; working with the news media; communications training; formal and informal opinion polls; and much more, depending on the organization.

Make communication a part of everything the organization does. Truly astute, forward-looking organizations often include effective communication among their goals and key objectives. Whatever our organization, we should ensure that open, honest, and strategic communication is supported by policy and considered important in the budget. Every objective should have a communications component that involves both listening to and sharing information and ideas. Communication, aimed at achieving the mission and keeping the organization in touch with staff, the community, and a world of ideas and opinions, should be a vital part of every school plan, curriculum adoption, job description, and evaluation.

The Communicator as Generalist

Every organization has a person with overall responsibility for communication. In many cases, a professional communication executive fills that post. If the slot isn't filled, then the next person up the line must take on this key leadership responsibility. It won't go away. Ultimately, everyone in an organization should be an outstanding communicator.

Communicators don't exist in a vacuum. They are, or should be, involved in all types and levels of activities. In an address to the national conference of the Public Relations Society of America (PRSA) in 1977, Frank Wylie, then the incoming president of the organization, said, "The public relations person must know far more than the professionals who work at more restrictive disciplines." The chief communicator "must be a well-informed generalist with a thorough knowledge of several specific fields ... and must have the judgment to place events, trends, and encounters into proper perspective." Each discipline earns its leadership role "through its ability to analyze, understand, anticipate, and predict" (Wylie, 1977).

16 Ideas and Techniques for Future-Focused Communication

We've mentioned the usual suspects—the newsletter, Web page, news media relations—and acknowledged that they are all important. However, they need to be part of a strategic approach to communication that is central to the whole process of staying in touch and creating a future. For those who have narrowed their definition of communication to "making us look good and fending off change," that may seem like a stretch.

In a fast-track world, however, we need to stretch even further. If we hope to develop a communication system that keeps us connected and moves us toward our vision, we should consider ideas and techniques—some quite broad in scope—that may or may not currently be on our list. Here are 16 such ideas and techniques, intended to stimulate further thinking:

1. Strategically defining and redefining culture
2. Constantly listening and scanning the environment
3. Developing and refreshing a strategic vision
4. Providing intellectual leadership
5. Engaging in generative thinking
6. Shaping or reshaping an identity or reputation
7. Managing perceptions and expectations
8. Dealing with pressure groups and criticism
9. Moving toward consensus
10. Preparing for crisis communication
11. Identifying and working with key communicators
12. Undertaking thematic efforts
13. Understanding social epidemiology
14. Forming an organic connection with those we serve
15. Conducting communications audits
16. Engaging in conceptual communication

The following sections cover each of these topics. All are important to the goal of becoming a connected leader capable of creating a future.

Strategically Defining and Redefining Culture

What is culture anyway? One definition describes it as "the integrated pattern of human knowledge, belief, and behavior that depends upon a person's capacity for learning and transmitting knowledge to succeeding generations" (*Webster's New Collegiate Dictionary*, 2004, p. 304).

People sometimes undergo "culture shock" when they are confused by situations that seem alien to them. Cultural anthropologists study and help us understand various aspects of culture, from social structure, language, and law to politics, art, religion, and technology. Too often we think of culture as only a reflection of race, ethnicity, or socioeconomic status. It is, but it's even bigger than that.

Educators are at the leading end of preparing students to become citizens of a highly diverse nation and world, a world of constant change. Therefore, they simply must understand the importance of cultural leadership and be engaged with the cultural melee. Internal and external cultures need to be at least somewhat compatible. That's possible only through strategic, culturally sensitive communication.

Cultural assets or anchors. To understand the phenomenon of cultural assets or anchors, let's look at two hypothetical extremes. In fact, education systems in various places and at various times might find themselves a part of either one.

- A *culture of mediocrity.* "Our community is losing jobs. The economy is not looking good. When our kids go off to college they never come back. Why go to the expense of educating them for somebody else? If these schools were good enough for me, they're good enough for them. Improving education just seems to backfire on us. Besides, with the money we've got, we have chuckholes to fill. People talk about becoming a number-one community. Forget it. We're forever number two, if that."

- A *culture of excellence and high expectations.* "Education is really the engine of our community. People want to come here because they know their children will get the kind of education that prepares them for the future. That's why our property values are going up, and it's why we're not only attracting but developing new industries. We expect a lot from our schools, and they expect a lot from us. I wouldn't want it any other way."

As educators, we want our staff and our community to define themselves by their commitment to outstanding education. While some education institutions pulsate with an expectation of excellence, others are faced with chronic failure of finance elections, torn by constant internal and external strife, and convinced they are victims who stand in the shadow of everyone else.

Are current internal and external cultures an asset, an anchor, or a potential anchor? The starting point for answering that question is a realistic assessment. If the culture, or certain aspects of it, is an asset, then the challenge will be to preserve those assets and not let them slip away, suggests Harvard Business School professor John Kotter. If the culture, or parts of it, turns out to be an anchor or a potential anchor that is holding us back from our highest aspirations, then, Kotter (2002) suggests, we're faced with a compelling question: "What actions can we take over time to turn our change-anchor culture into a more adaptive culture?" He admits that "creating an adaptive culture ... is never easy ... but the alternative is to be pulverized by an increasingly turbulent environment" (p. 177).

Redefining the culture. Often, leaders apply what they consider their best management techniques to improving an organization and seem to get absolutely nowhere. The problem could be that those "improvements" are simply incompatible with a culture that is stuck in the status quo.

How can we help a community or a staff redefine its culture? First, to better understand the sea in which we swim, we should use the processes described earlier in this book to scan the environment and to start the conversation about a vision for the future. Get beyond the pessimism, which is often based on history and grim reality, by asking people to probe their highest aspirations. Forget for a few hours the chains that pin us against the wall of our narrow cell and make us a captive of our "it's no use" mentality. Start to dream, and ask, "If we were setting audacious goals, what might they be?"

Then, in our communication, we should reflect those high aspirations back to our community. What do we want to become? What are our dreams for the future? How would we like to have others describe our community, our school system, our college, university, or other organization? How can we get from where we are to where we want to be?

Keeping people well informed is bread and butter. However, our communication should also be tied to broad-based strategies that compel us to be sensitive to ongoing change and help us build, shape, define, and maintain a culture of excellence. Our success may very well depend on how we affect the culture of the organization and the community we serve.

School climate and culture. Frequently, thoughtful observers make direct connections between the climate in a school and the culture of its surrounding community. Most educators want to achieve a winning school climate, because they know it is a key correlate of effective schools. The culture of the community can make achieving an even better school climate easier or more difficult.

Jim Sweeney, a longtime distinguished professor at Iowa State University who conducted school-climate studies in hundreds of schools and worked with thousands of teachers, points out 10 factors that are essential to a winning school climate (1991, p. 1):

1. A supportive, stimulating environment
2. Student-centeredness

3. Positive expectations
4. Feedback
5. Rewards
6. A sense of family
7. Closeness to parents and community
8. Communication
9. Achievement
10. Trust

Constantly Listening and Scanning the Environment

Whatever magnificent specialist skills we may have, we also need to see things in context. Otherwise, we are destined to deal with what we might see as a deluge of disconnected dilemmas. Rather than viewing what's happening as part of a larger whole, we fight the pieces, often not seeing that our "solution" to one problem creates another concern somewhere else.

Staying in touch requires a constant program of systematic listening and scanning the internal and external environments. Through formal and informal opinion polls, get-togethers with people at a local restaurant, advisory councils, parent organization meetings, and a host of other means, we try to stay close to those we serve.

Complete chapters of this book have been devoted to each of several techniques for mobilizing the listening and scanning process. For the sake of convenience, we'll review some of them here, since each is energized by future-focused leadership and communication. Each makes a distinct contribution to defining the internal and external cultures, and all are a part of strategic communication.

- **Trends.** Identify trends and their implications for your profession, industry, organization, or perhaps nation or world.
- **Issues.** Engage a broad range of people in identifying issues and helping to sort them according to their probability and impact.

Consider which are critical, ongoing, or emerging issues, and the priority each should be assigned.

- **PEST/STEEPV.** Tap the ingenuity of the staff and community in identifying political, economic, social, and technological (PEST) forces that might and perhaps should affect how we run the organization. Add environmental forces and values to develop a STEEPV analysis. Also think about the impact those forces might have on what students will need to know and be able to do to be prepared for the future.

- **SWOT.** Analyze the strengths, weaknesses, opportunities, and threats (SWOT) facing the organization and consider their implications for the future.

- **Gap analysis.** Engage people in developing statements that describe what they consider an ideal or desirable organization or community. Rate each statement, perhaps on a scale of 1 to 5 or 1 to 10, in comparison to current realities. Consider the differences, and, as they say on the London subways, "Mind the gap."

- **Root cause and defining moments analysis.** Have people identify what they consider defining moments in the life of the organization or root causes that contributed to current problems or successes.

- **Flexibility/innovation analysis.** Consider how flexible the staff and community are in terms of changes that might be needed to move the organization into a global knowledge/information age.

- **Formal and informal questionnaires/surveys.** Regularly, through mailed or e-mailed questionnaires or phone and personal contact, ask people to express their opinions. Find out what they know, what they don't know, what they understand and misunderstand, how deeply they feel about an issue, what their needs are, and how well they think those needs are being met.

- **Demographics.** Do constant research on the demographics of students, staff, and the community to better understand racial, ethnic, social, and economic factors.

- **Psychographics.** Although there is a tendency to group people by their demographic characteristics, people within those groups are increasingly identifying themselves based on what motivates them, their values, or their views on a variety of issues. Use a combination of approaches to develop a better understanding of the culture of the organization and the community, to help target communication, and to provide a base of information and guidance for *reinforcing* certain aspects of the culture and *transforming* others.

Developing and Refreshing a Strategic Vision

Vision can have many meanings. Philosopher and Harvard University professor Edward O. Wilson (1998) describes vision in a broad and literal sense when he notes that, with the aid of special microscopes and telescopes, we can now "peer downward to the trajectories of subatomic particles and outward to star birth in distant galaxies whose incoming light dates back to the beginning of the universe" (pp. 46–47). Here the reference is to a strategic vision for an organization, such as a school system or college; an industry, such as education; a community; or even a country.

Working with staff and the community, educators need to provide leadership for creating a constantly evolving vision for the future. The same is true for people in the for-profit sector, whose leadership in creating a vision may reach out to a community that includes employees, customers, suppliers, and a host of others.

Using special tools and processes, we can involve a diverse group of people in developing a vision, or a description, of the future we would like to see. These tools and processes (described in some depth in Chapters 7 and 8) are driven by strategic, future-focused leadership and communication. They might include identifying the characteristics of the organization we want to become and developing and considering scenarios.

Reaching broad-based agreement on a vision is a bold step in defining or redefining an organization's or a community's culture. Vision and mission statements should be complementary. They should help us define how we see our role as we move into the future, consider the reasons for our existence, and identify the primary forces that drive us.

A case in point is a mission statement and a set of future-oriented goals adopted by the Pennsylvania School Boards Association (PSBA) in 2004. The first states that the mission of the association is "to promote excellence in school board governance through leadership, service, and advocacy for public education." Among the goals is a commitment to "continue to engage PSBA members and others in envisioning and shaping the future of public education." This is just one example of a process involving informed environmental scanning and visioning brought to life.

Providing Intellectual Leadership

Educators and others who hold key positions in society should be expected to be intellectual leaders. What are the qualities of an intellectual leader? An intellectual leader is a person who is in touch with the issues, sees things in context, can clearly explain both the big and little pictures, demonstrates both critical and creative thinking skills, and understands the meaning of what's going on around us.

The true intellectual leader is an interdependent generalist. People who understand that fact of life know that strategic, future-focused communication and intellectual leadership go hand-in-hand.

Engaging in Generative Thinking

Sometimes we get so caught up in the finality of our discussion—in reaching decisions, setting policies, selecting programs, or deciding on a course of action—that we leave little time for creative thought. As part of the decision-making process, we need to tap the genius of people—those we depend on and those we serve. An earlier suggestion recommended sharing information about societal trends and then encouraging people to brainstorm about the possible implications of those trends for how we run the organization and what we teach. The idea behind brainstorming, a form of generative thinking, is simple: To the extent possible, let's get the ideas on the table first and decide later, if we want to decide at all.

Rick Smyre, president of the Center for Communities of the Future, is a champion of generative thinking. He believes, for example, that leaders should engage people in identifying questions that need to be asked. Then he suggests "futures generative dialogue," based on the idea that "diverse people in an organization or community will need to learn how to collaborate and connect at a deeper level in multiple intersecting processes of innovation." Smyre notes that "without the ability to see value in what others say, and without the capacity to think about issues within a futures context, there will be few truly innovative approaches that emerge to ensure that people, organizations, and communities remain vital and sustainable" (2004, p. 3).

True leaders are not threatened by ideas. Instead, they are constantly engaging broad circles of people in the process of generative thinking. They believe that genius can spring from anyone, despite differences in demographic characteristics or values. They also understand the principles of complexity theory and know that constantly staying close to the thinking of others, keeping an ear to the ground, will help them put even the surprises into context. A 21st century leader is capable of dealing with ambiguity and finds discontinuity downright exciting, a breeding ground for new ideas and opportunities.

Shaping or Reshaping an Identity or Reputation

How would people describe you, your organization, and your industry today? How would you like them to describe you? What would you want people to say about your organization behind your back? What are the characteristics of a school system, college, or university that is capable of preparing students for the future?

To legitimately justify the identity we'd like to achieve, we need to consider both how we operate and how we communicate. Rather than fighting to the death to defend the status quo, we need to loosen up and consider what we can or should become.

Obviously, just to keep up, we'll need to constantly rethink how we define ourselves. A 1970s identity may not work in a 21st century world unless the goal is to capitalize on nostalgia. Thirty-year-old policies might inhibit progress and actually keep education systems and communities from maintaining essential links with a world that is constantly in motion. Our identity and our reputation are inseparable and an essential part of future-focused leadership and communication.

Complexity Theory

What have new technologies wrought? We know for sure that they've accelerated the pace of change. It's also no secret that they have increased the complexity of what we might already have thought was a chaotic environment.

According to Megan Santosus (1998), writing in *CIO Enterprise* magazine, "Complexity theorists argue that managers should allow creativity and efficiency to emerge naturally within organizations rather than imposing their own solutions on their employees. They can do this by setting some basic ground rules and then encouraging interactions or relationships among their employees so that solutions emerge from the bottom up."

In an interview for Santosus's article, Roger Lewin, author of *Complexity: Life on the Edge of Chaos,* comments, "Traditionally, business people think about their worlds in a very mechanistic, linear way that is characterized by simple cause and effect and is predictable." Lewin emphasizes, "Most of the world isn't like that. Complexity theory looks at these systems in ways that are organic, nonlinear, and holistic."

In short, the simple rules aren't that simple anymore. Rather than let complexity overwhelm us, we need to get a handle on the complexity.

Managing Perceptions and Expectations

An *environmental scan* will give us some idea about the perceptions people currently have of our organization. The *visioning process* will help us identify the perceptions we'd like them to have. Then, as mentioned several times in this book, we need to develop a substantive plan to get us from where we are to where we want to be. Managing the constellation of expectations that students, parents, teachers, administrators, board members, businesspeople, governments, and others have for each other is an ongoing challenge. Strategic communication should help these and other groups develop, to the extent possible, mutual expectations.

Dealing with Pressure Groups and Criticism

Because we are concerned about leadership that will help us prepare the education institution and its students for the future, not freeze them in the past, we will likely be nudging against treasured opinions, values, biases, beliefs, and lifestyles. Change is never easy.

In dealing with pressure groups and criticism, we need to check our own beliefs. For example, pressure groups are not abnormal. They are a key component of a free and democratic society. The First Amendment to the U.S. Constitution protects the individual right to dissent. Understanding how to deal with conflicting points of view is basic to being truly prepared for strategic, future-focused communication.

Here are a few tips for working with pressure groups:

- Deal with representatives of pressure groups openly and honestly.
- Get together for a visit with an individual or small group. Try to clear the air and get rid of myths.
- Keep in mind that, in many cases, members of the group will only want to have their voices heard.
- Seek a common denominator, if one can be found.

- Be adaptable, if adaptability is reasonable.
- Apply techniques of negotiation. Communicate well and apply consensus-building techniques.
- Be sure that everyone who needs to know is immediately informed of your contacts with representatives of a pressure group.
- Be a good listener. Try to determine the issue, concern, problem, or motive, whether stated or unstated.

The following are a few considerations for dealing with criticism:

- Stay close to the environment through surveys and the regular involvement of people. Always be listening.
- Seek support in advance by engaging people in the decision-making process.
- Operate as a team. Keep key individuals and groups informed about how you handled a situation.
- Be aware of nonverbal messages, which may help you understand the criticism.
- Never ask for advice if you will not consider it.
- Be consistent, and avoid half-truths.

Moving Toward Consensus

Although full agreement—total consensus—is seldom possible in a free and democratic society, we do want to move toward legitimate decisions that are as inclusive as possible. We want people to feel comfortable under the tent.

Consensus building calls for at least a basic understanding of how people work together in groups. For example, in many groups, there are *controlling communicators*, who are not interested in other people's ideas, only their own; *withdrawn communicators*, who have little or nothing to add to the discussion; *relinquishing communicators*, who simply go along with someone else in the group or someone not even in the room whose views they have adopted; and *developmental communicators,* who are eager to hear everyone's views and draw statements that come close to reflecting a consensus of the group. Whenever possible, connected leaders need to play the role of developmental communicator.

Preparing for Crisis Communication

Without exception, every organization needs a crisis plan. Whether the crisis comes as a complete surprise or represents the intended or unintended consequences of something we have or have not said or done, we need to be ready.

Development of that plan should involve a broad cross-section of staff and community. The plan should be continuously updated and communicated—even rehearsed. Crisis-management teams should be identified and know their responsibilities.

What might be included in a crisis plan? Here are some components (Marx, 2001):

- Reasons for the plan; why it is needed
- The types of crises covered by the plan, including checklists for each
- Emergency telephone numbers
- Detailed maps of each facility
- Procedural information, including guidelines for closings, lockdowns, or evacuations, and codes to serve as shorthand for various types of crises, such as Code 1, Code 2, or Code 3
- Guidelines for effective communication with media, staff, and the community

Safety and security are a primary concern, because it's hard to teach or learn if we're constantly looking over our shoulders, expecting the worst. A crisis plan could actually help prevent a crisis from becoming a catastrophe.

From the standpoint of leadership, the plan will be a source of confidence for the community during a time of tragedy or uncertainty. Many leaders anticipate what they might be able to say in the wake of an unexpected tragedy when a reporter asks, "What did you do to prevent this?" The plan can help provide that answer, when leadership is on the line and the world may be watching.

How we handle crises can leave a lasting impression about our leadership and communication skills. If we handle them reasonably well, we're very likely to enjoy higher levels of trust as we move toward creating a future for our organization and our students. It's also important to remember that the process of change can, in itself, create occasional crises.

Identifying and Working with Key Communicators

This approach to communication has grown in acceptance over several decades. Key people, whom others rely on for information, are identified and kept in the loop. They may be reporters; city, county, and other officials; people with a particular interest in education; hairdressers; cab drivers; involved parents; service club members; older citizens, including retirees from the school system or college; alumni; and many others. The concept is that if we share the information with them, they will share it with others.

The key-communicator process has become more efficient with the advent of Web sites and e-mail, because people can now choose their areas of deepest interest, and related information can be sent to them instantly.

One way to start putting together lists of key communicators is to identify the leadership of various business, government, education, and other groups. Another is to ask people, "Who would you turn to for information about what's going on in the school system?" Key communicators can help us get to the very root of the grapevine.

Undertaking Thematic Efforts

When we've decided on our philosophical direction, we need to develop a theme that honestly reflects what we're trying to accomplish. Of course, that theme should be a basic part of our future-focused communication plan.

A sound theme is not just a slogan. It actually reflects what we are honestly striving to achieve. An effective theme should be short, rhythmic, memorable, and conceptual. It should not be a smokescreen or a substitute for substantive action. Consider themes that support ongoing, future-oriented efforts, such as "Getting Better for Kids" or "Education: The Best Investment We Can Make in Our Future."

Understanding Social Epidemiology

Theodore Gordon, senior research fellow at the Millennium Project and founder of the Futures Group, coined the term "social epidemiology" for an idea that many thoughtful people have been discussing for some time. The point is that some ideas can spread like viruses. They may be latent, waiting to be discovered and to have someone make them "contagious" (Gordon, 2003b).

Malcolm Gladwell, in his now-celebrated book *The Tipping Point: How Little Things Can Make a Big Difference* (2002), touts the influence of Paul Revere, when he made his famous ride on April 18, 1775. Galloping through the countryside, he cried, "The British are coming." Revere was like social glue. People knew him and trusted him, and they turned out in droves to defend their fledgling nation. Paul Revere had started what Gladwell calls "a word-of-mouth epidemic" (p. 32). As architects of the future, we need to understand how important it is to develop ideas that are so connected and so compelling that they will spread, leading to an even more dynamic and effective organization.

Forming an Organic Connection with Those We Serve

Famed architect Frank Lloyd Wright designed his structures to have an organic connection with the environment. To bring a structure and its environment into harmony, he considered three things—materials, site, and client. Although each of those terms may take on a different meaning, depending on where we are and what we do, Wright's approach gives us an easy-to-understand insight into how we can get connected to the world around us. The processes described in this book are specifically designed to help us make our education institutions and our programs even more organically connected to the needs of our environment.

Conducting Communications Audits

Occasionally, to gain opinions about how a communications program can become more strategic, organizations sponsor an audit. Representatives of key publics are generally asked to respond to interviews or questionnaires.

An audit will often suggest how communication can become even more central to any organization's ultimate success. It can help determine how well traditional forms of communication are fulfilling the needs of the organization and its internal and external publics. The audit could also suggest how those efforts can become more future-focused.

Engaging in Conceptual Communication

Consider the information available on any topic. Often it's voluminous, and it's increasing exponentially. To communicate all of it may simply overwhelm people and actually turn them off. As strategic, future-focused communicators, we need to consider what seems like a truckload of information, or a flurry of sometimes conflicting stories or events, and reduce it to a basic concept. Entire speeches, articles, and books can be reduced to concepts such as these: "Education is an investment, not an expense," "We all benefit from education," or "We can't afford the cost of neglect."

Although most organizations are good at communicating the "who, what, when, where, and how," they are often weak on the "why." To help people truly understand a program or a proposal, we need to deliberately communicate what it means to them—why we're making certain recommendations or doing what we're doing. In short, we need to consider how we will communicate *meaning*, not just information. Here are 12 suggestions for how to communicate meaning:

1. **Be eloquent.** Think of Martin Luther King Jr.'s "I have a dream" speech. Make what you're saying memorable. Eloquence might be described as the colorful expression of intellect.

2. **Use standards as a measuring stick.** "Here are the standards. This is the code of ethics we considered in making our decision or in developing our recommendation." This approach lets people know that what you're presenting didn't simply come out of thin air.

3. **Use startling facts.** In communication, the first step is generally getting attention. "In the wealthiest nation on earth, 16 percent of children under age six live in poverty." It's facts such as that one that cause people to sit up and take notice.

4. **Use a numbered list.** Whether it's the Ten Commandments or the Four Freedoms, any list that is numbered is more memorable than a list that isn't.

5. **Use comparisons and contrasts.** Some things are simply easier to understand when we compare or contrast them with something else. "For what that thing cost the government, we could have provided total funding for 200 average-sized school districts. Which would have given the best return on our investment?"

6. **Point out conflict.** In some cases, we can describe the situation only by pointing out the conflict we're facing. "We have a few cases of _____. The Centers for Disease Control has said that it is

not easily spread. We've taken all the suggested precautions. Those are the facts. On the other hand, many students and their parents are still quite concerned. We're caught in a conflict, or tug-of-war, between fear and fact."

7. **Show connections.** By understanding key publics, we'll be able to show the connection between a proposal and its possible impact on what is of greatest interest to certain individuals or groups.

8. **Show benefits.** A bottom-line question people will ask, whether aloud or not, is "What's in this for me?" As a businessperson or as an older citizen, "How will I benefit from this?" One way to get an answer to those types of questions is to bring people together, present a proposal, and ask them to identify "what's in it for them."

9. **Use lateral thinking.** Sometimes we need to move from critical to creative thinking and demonstrate our ability to think outside the box. We need to come up with unconventional solutions to what are often unconventional challenges.

10. **Reframe the issue.** Because there are frequently more than five sides to every issue, not just two, we have an opportunity to reframe. Consider an idea framed in this way: "Education is the problem." Now consider it reframed in this way: "Education is not the problem. Education is the solution to problems society has created for us."

11. **Use debate techniques.** Although debate techniques need to be applied with humility and a great deal of grace, it is possible to use them in communicating clarity. For example, someone might refute a point that you've spent substantial time researching. Your response might be, "Thank you. Let me show you how what you've just presented actually strengthens what we're recommending." For the record, that's called "utilizing."

12. **Be wise, conceptualize.** We've discussed the importance of reducing masses of information to a brief concept that instantly communicates an idea or fact. For example, when one school system was faced with combining schools because enrollments had dropped

by thousands of students, it presented its case under the concept of "Pulling Together for Kids."

The Inseparability of Strategic Communication and Leadership

Leaders do more than manage. They define, stimulate, shape, and build support for ideas and processes that make an organization compatible with its highest calling. Some have deep knowledge in certain specialties, but they are also generalists who help people around them see what's happening in a broader context. Strategic, future-focused communication and leadership are inseparable.

In a chaotic and complex world, ideas come at us from every direction. As leaders, a good part of what we do is encourage people to find interrelationships and interdependencies among those ideas. When that happens, the static becomes the dynamic. Synergy sets in, and we become greater than the sum of our parts. In essence, strategic communication goes far beyond simply telling people what we want them to know or think.

In the Drucker Foundation book *The Community of the Future,* Rita Sussmuth (1998) warns of reactions to our attempts to involve people in the process of creating a vibrant, future-oriented organization. She refers to our move from an industrial to an information society as the "Bit Bang." Sussmuth comments that the changes are so breathtaking that they might trigger "not only visions but also uncertainty and apprehensions, which are often associated with a withdrawal to smaller and more manageable units." Therefore, leaders will be pressed to guarantee the sincerity and motivations of their efforts to avoid what Sussmuth sees as "a fear of manipulation and social alienation" (pp. 30–31).

Peter Senge, director of the Center for Organizational Learning at the Massachusetts Institute of Technology, believes learning organizations, with people constantly sharing and learning from each other, are a key to a brighter future. "Sharing knowledge occurs when people are genuinely interested in helping one another develop new capacities for action; it is about creating learning processes" (2002, pp. 136–137).

A gentle reminder: Because of educators' important role in society, anyone involved in education is, or should be, a leader. Strategic, future-focused leadership and communication is not confined to the executive office. It's everybody's job.

Questions and Activities

1. Considering your institution, develop a basic plan for strategic communication. What should be included that goes beyond "traditional but necessary" methods for communication?
2. Read the portions of this chapter that address complexity or chaos theory. How might your organization need to change to be effective in this type of fast-changing environment?
3. Ask a group of people to read this chapter and then engage them in responding to these questions: How are we communicating now? How should we be communicating?

Readings

Bagin, D., & Gallagher, D. R. (2001). *The school and community relations*. Needham Heights, MA: Allyn and Bacon.

Gibson, R. (Ed.). (2002). *Rethinking the future*. London: Nicholas Brealey Publishing.

Gladwell, M. (2002). *The tipping point: How little things can make a big difference*. Boston: Back Bay Books.

National School Public Relations Association. [Assorted publications]. Rockville, MD: Author.

Wilson, E. O. (1998). *Consilience: The unity of knowledge*. New York: Knopf.

PART 5

Moving Forward

As we've thought about creating a future, we've considered the importance of connected leaders. We've explored how to stay close to the internal and external environments and taken first steps in the direction of defining a vision. To make sure we have the support we need and that our efforts are understood, we've reviewed tools and techniques for future-focused communication. Now the time has come to engage people in the process. Chapter 10 zeroes in on how to get the ball rolling.

10 | Getting the Ball Rolling

A journey of a thousand miles begins with a single step.

—Chinese proverb

Remember when a strategic plan was developed every three to five years and people were then expected to simply follow it? Having the plan is as important as ever. However, today and into the future, pursuing the plan and ignoring the surrounding world simply won't work. Fluidity is in. Rigidity is out.

Flexibility should be built into the strategic plan and understood in the mission of the organization. Of course, adhering to guiding principles is important, but surviving and legitimately pursuing the mission requires firming up ongoing connections with a diversity of people, information, and ideas. When we do that, we become increasingly comfortable with the stark fact that what worked yesterday may not be adequate for tomorrow.

Continuous improvement is an energizing concept, and it's a necessity for any organization that hopes to thrive—even survive—in the future. As leaders, our commitment to continuous improvement can help us take a quantum leap toward becoming strategic futurists who play an essential, entrepreneurial, and intellectual leadership role in our communities. Principled people who are open to a constantly accelerating flow of ideas stake out the higher ground. They demonstrate that they have *earned* the position of leader, not simply declared it.

So, how can we get the ball rolling?

Two-Track, Parallel Planning

A two-track planning process can help constantly renew the organization. On the one hand is a group that develops, monitors, and updates the actual plan. On the other are diverse groups of people who regularly engage in generative thinking, freely sharing their ideas and helping create an even more viable system. Together, the two components provide parallel planning.

Plans should always be informed by the constant inflow of information and ideas. Granted, any group is capable of thinking about the future. However, unless we develop a systematic way of listening—of tapping the ingenuity of the staff and community and connecting with the forces affecting society—we'll very likely find ourselves out of touch and behind the curve. The following are some steps to put the ideas in this book to work:

Make it clear that all educators are leaders by virtue of the important role they play in society. Encourage teachers, administrators, board members, parent and community leaders, and others to read this book. Help them understand their role as connected leaders and the importance of staying in touch with societal forces that affect education organizations, educators, and students.

Regularly engage all staff in the process of scanning the environment. At occasional faculty, departmental, cabinet, board, and other meetings, devote agenda time to identifying and considering the implications of trends and issues. Make it clear to both education and support staff that the focus is on the future, because that is where students will live their lives.

Make environmental scanning and visioning tools and techniques a part of "how we do business." When you do a formal update of your plan, reviewing your vision and mission and setting your goals, inform the process by using the tools and techniques described in this book. However, understand that these tools and techniques—spotting political, economic, social, and technological forces affecting the organization; identifying and sorting issues; considering the gap between where the organization is and where you'd like it to be; and thinking about root causes of problems you may be facing—can help in your everyday work, at all levels. Ongoing, strategic, future-focused leadership and communication are the foundation of any truly successful organization.

Set up a futures council or a network of them. These 15- to 20-member groups are strictly advisory, composed of both staff and community, and may meet a couple of times a year. They have frequently rotating memberships to engage increasing numbers of people. Members are charged with generative thinking that will help the organization adjust to accelerating change. Those involved in these councils understand from the outset that they are not to use the forum to promote a single issue or for ax grinding.

These ad hoc futures councils help identify trends and issues. They also study trends, such as the ones listed in this book.

Agendas might include the following components: (1) an explanation of the council's generative-thinking, advisory role; (2) a presentation on trends and issues; (3) identification of additional trends and issues the group thinks might be emerging; and (4) small-group brainstorming sessions focused on identifying the possible implications of certain trends or issues for the education system, for what students need to know and be able to do to be prepared for the future, for economic growth and development, or for quality-of-life issues in the community. Occasionally, speakers may appear before the group for updates on trends that might be developing.

Collect, share, and consider the ideas generated by futures councils. Implications of trends and issues identified by these councils are shared with the communications department, planning office, school superintendent or college president's office, an ad hoc planning advisory council, or someone else who is designated to summarize the thinking generated at these sessions. Then these summaries are shared at regular leadership council, departmental, planning, or other meetings. In reviewing the items, ongoing questions might include these: Should this idea affect the way we conduct business?

Do we need to adjust our plan and possibly our policies to accommodate these changes in the environment? What impact should this idea have on what we teach and how we teach it?

Conduct staff and community surveys. Periodic surveys generally involve more representatives of the staff and community, though they can be used to generate the same type of thinking that takes place at futures council meetings. This type of involvement can reveal further trends and issues for direct consideration by the organization or by the councils.

Make the process continuous. Even though they will frequently engage new members, the futures councils are not a one-shot deal. Instead, these thoughtful groups help generate a continuous stream of fresh thinking and insights and help the organization maintain fluidity that will support ongoing innovation and renewal. They will become part of an ongoing process for keeping the organization on the leading edge of the future.

This approach is purposely open-ended. It does not provide all the answers. The names of these councils might vary. In some communities, a single, larger futures council might make more sense than several smaller ones.

Local policy will determine who makes appointments to these councils and the length of members' terms of service. In some cases, the membership might rotate from one meeting to the next to engage the thinking of even more people. Decisions will need to be made about when and how information and ideas from these groups are reported to the board, staff, and community. Facilitators will be needed to ensure there is brainstorming of ideas that will benefit the system in the future rather than rehashing of gripes.

Educators may encounter other community and business leaders who would like to use the same futures council or similar groups to consider the implications of trends and issues for economic growth and development or community-wide improvement. When that happens, the education system has truly earned its coveted position as a positive, essential, and future-oriented force in the total life of the community.

Futures Studies

If we truly believe in the importance of developing connected leaders capable of constantly creating a sustainable future, if we hope to encourage individuals and generations of people to use their imaginations to move us in the direction of creative, daring, and audacious goals, then we need to support futures studies in our schools and colleges. The same leadership skills, the same tools and techniques for scanning the environment and developing a vision of the future, and the same strategies we've discussed for effective communication can enliven any course, help us reshape how we think about education, and make active learning a reality. These components can also be combined in courses or units called "Futures Studies." Consider this: If you were developing a futures studies course, what would it include?

Pooling Ingenuity

The staff and community of every school, school system, college, or other organization is a resource filled with ideas and energy. Too often that resource is untapped and underappreciated.

People talk about synergy. The type of listening and responding described in this book can make synergy happen, and it provides a genuine example of democracy at work. When people are involved, when they are asked for their ideas and opinions, they will have a greater sense of ownership for the organization and what it's trying to accomplish. When an education system uses an inclusive approach that engages people in shaping the future, it sends a strong signal that the education system is the crossroads and central convening point for the community.

Creating a future is, after all, the essence of leadership.

Questions and Activities

1. Based on this final chapter and the ideas reflected throughout this book, develop a two-page paper describing how you would engage

in a two-track planning process, involving both development of an actual plan and generative thinking.

2. What do we mean when we say, "Rigidity is out. Fluidity is in."?

3. Develop a preliminary syllabus for a futures studies course.

Readings

Gelb, M. J. (1998). *How to think like Leonardo da Vinci*. New York: Dell Publishing.

Appendix A

Additional Examples of Issues from the Advisory Council

The following are additional examples of issues facing education identified by the Creating a Future Advisory Council. This distinguished group, whose names are listed in the Acknowledgments section, provided advice in developing this publication. Additional representative examples are found in Chapter 5, which is devoted to issue management.

Closing the achievement gap is an ongoing challenge. "Many in America do not have the will or the desire to address this issue. In the suburbs, where I am, the public does not expect excuses. They expect the ongoing delivery of high-quality programs and high achievement." —*Keith Marty, superintendent, School District of Menomonee Falls, Wisconsin*

Legislators have intervened to overwhelm the authority of educators—to set academic standards—but without regard for new ways to organize learning and new ways to make it more productive and successful for children with more kinds of learning styles. "With powerful software and media that provably work, why aren't we thinking about ways to redistribute costs to create more effective resources? Learning can be more efficient and proceed at a faster pace, perhaps reducing the number of days of seat time required to move on to higher education." —*Gary Rowe, president, Rowe Inc., Lawrenceville, Georgia*

School districts lack infrastructure to provide services schools need to meet the learning needs of students. "Most districts do not have a data-management system in place to give teachers immediate and ongoing information on how their students are achieving on standards. Without this information, it is much more difficult to align instruction to the students' needs." —*Jane Hammond, superintendent-in-residence, Stupski Foundation, Mill Valley, California, and a veteran school superintendent*

Student assessment may be overemphasized as a means to improve the education system. "Lack of funding, coupled with a misdirected focus on testing results and expanded expectations placed on schools, can be a recipe for failure. Appropriate funding, building and focusing on teaching inputs and the learning process, can lead to meeting all learners' needs." —*Kenneth Bird, superintendent, The Westside Community Schools, Omaha, Nebraska*

The funding of public education is inadequate to meet the demands of current policy standards. "Public schools educate the majority of American students. As it becomes more challenging to fund schools adequately, the need to totally reform the funding infrastructure of public schools will become more critical and of greater public interest." —*Marc Ecker, 2003–04 president, National Middle School Association, and superintendent, Fountain Valley, California*

There is a lack of equity in education for all children. "The negative impact on students attending schools in poor districts has been documented with numerous studies. Many school systems are struggling financially to meet several new mandates of No Child Left Behind. As a classroom teacher, I welcome the accountability of this legislation, but I understand the financial strain this is creating for many. In order for all children, including those from low-income families, to have safe, healthy, and comfortable school facilities with well-qualified teachers and high-quality curriculum and learning materials, we all must work together. Federal, state, and local governments, along with educators, parents, and citizens, all need to become stakeholders in our schools." —*Betsy Rogers, teacher, Jefferson County Public Schools, Birmingham, Alabama, and 2003 National Teacher of the Year*

The relatively low status of education department degrees at institutions of higher learning needs to be enhanced, requiring an accompanying enhancement of professional prestige, status, earnings, and rewards. "Failing to provide every student with proper and best opportunities for honing and developing their innermost potentials is a tragedy." —*Graham T. T. Molitor, president, Public Policy Forecasting, and vice president and legal counsel, World Future Society, Bethesda, Maryland*

In order to ensure the relevancy of teacher preparation programs, curricula must include survival skills, in addition to subject knowledge and pedagogy. "Higher education programs should reflect the National Board for Professional Teaching Standards reflective practitioner approach to ensure the newest (and most vulnerable) educators are adequately prepared for the new school environment with its diverse student body. Mentoring programs are important for new and beginning teachers." —*Drew Albritten, executive director, The Council for Exceptional Children, Arlington, Virginia*

State budgets continue to be cause for concern. "Most state education agencies are understaffed, underfunded, and underappreciated. Special initiatives that might help address/ameliorate the student achievement gap are defunded or receive reduced funding, such as after-school programs, in-school tutoring programs, school reform models, and so on. The achievement gap continues, widens, and deepens. Hardened attitudes about 'those people' become even harder. The testing continues." —*Elizabeth L. Hale, president, Institute for Educational Leadership, Washington, D.C.*

Schools are becoming specialized, as seen in the growth of charter, private, and home schooling to meet specialized market niches. "As schools are perceived as failing and budget cuts are constantly in the headlines, parents and students will look elsewhere to meet their needs. Most of the options available to students leaving the public schools have a decidedly narrow focus when contrasted with the American common school that was conceptually designed over 200 years ago to meet the needs of all youngsters who appeared at the schoolhouse door." —*Ted Blaesing, superintendent, White Bear Lake Area Schools, White Bear Lake, Minnesota*

The uneasy connections between secondary and postsecondary education need to be resolved. "The technical issues to improve transitions will move to resolution when there is better agreement on a mission for near-universal success." —*Ted Stilwill, former director, Iowa Department of Education, Des Moines, Iowa*

Appendix B

A Checklist for Creating and Working with a Futures Council

Consider the benefits of an ongoing futures council, not as a decision-making body, but as an ear to the ground, a way of getting a constant stream of thinking and advice from a diverse group of constituents. Actually, an education institution or any other type of organization might have a number of these councils with rotating memberships to help them tap the thinking of a broad cross-section of people.

These types of councils can engage in generative thinking at the organizational, system, school, campus, departmental, or other level. Futures councils might also be ready-made to participate in some of the processes for environmental scanning discussed in Chapters 3 and 6.

The following checklist can help with the formation of futures councils:

☐ Identify a diverse group or groups made up of staff and community to engage in generative thinking. Make it clear that the group's activities will be strictly advisory. In addition to the name "Futures Council," other names might include "Trends Council" or "Vision Council."

☐ Ask a respected and capable member of the community to serve as chair of the council. This person should understand and respect the group's advisory role.

☐ Inform the group about its responsibility and provide members with printed information and Web sites that will inform their discussions. Consider inviting a futurist to discuss societal trends with a broad cross-section of the staff and community.

☐ Engage the council, or an even more inclusive group, in a full- or half-day meeting. (Another approach would be to have the council hold meetings, a few hours each, a couple of times a year.)

☐ Schedule the meeting at a venue that has special significance in the community.

☐ At that meeting, in a highly facilitated process, ask the council to engage in one or more environmental scanning processes, such as identifying and speculating on the implication of trends or considering the political, economic, social, and technological forces affecting society and their possible impacts on education and the community.

☐ Summarize the ideas generated during the meeting or meetings.

☐ Consider developing a questionnaire, distributed by regular mail or e-mail, to gain further insights from an expanded group about trends and other forces identified at the meeting and about items that might have been missed.

☐ Appoint a representative Staff Trends Action Team to work with the Futures Council in developing a list of possible approaches for addressing the trends and other societal forces that have been identified.

☐ Consider those possibilities in the development of vision and mission statements, plans, goals, and objectives, and ask everyone to consider how the information might be used to make current programs even more effective.

☐ Share the results of the effort with the broader community to stimulate thinking about the future, to encourage support for needed advancements, to let people know that the system is dynamic and open to ideas, to support constant development of a living strategy, to guide the board in making decisions, and to build a culture that finds excitement and even pride in the constant process of creating a future.

Appendix C
A State of the Future Index

To stretch our thinking about environmental scanning and using the results, let's consider how we might develop an index, reflecting key factors, to help us gauge our progress over time. Although the following example is not directly related to education, it can be used to develop a similar index for education. A key question might be: "What would be included in a State of Education Index?"

Theodore Gordon, senior research fellow for the Millennium Project at the American Council for the United Nations University and founder of The Futures Group, is a longtime leader in scanning the environment and bringing it into sharper focus. In 2001–02, the Millennium Project's research program began "an investigation into the development and potential use of a State of the Future Index (SOFI)" (Gordon, 2003b). The index would include "an experimental approach to the statistical combination of historical records and forecasts of selected global indicators." Although the "apparent precision of an index can easily be mistaken for accuracy," Gordon pointed out, the SOFI could serve as an indicator of progress and problems in various parts of the world.

Gordon noted five key questions crucial to the development of an appropriate index:

1. What variables should be included in the index?
2. How can very different variables be combined?
3. How can the variables be forecast?
4. How can the variables be weighted?
5. How can double accounting be avoided? (For example, carbon dioxide concentrations and global temperature might provide highly related information.)

After surveying 600 futurists and scholars in 50 countries, the project settled on the following variables to be included in the index:

- Infant mortality rate
- Food availability
- Gross National Product per capita
- Households with access to fresh water
- Carbon dioxide emissions
- Annual population addition
- Percent unemployed
- Literacy rate (adult total)
- Annual AIDS deaths
- Life expectancy
- Number of armed conflicts
- Developing-country debt
- Forestlands
- Rich/poor gap
- Terrorist attacks
- Violent crime rate
- Population in countries that are not free
- Secondary school enrollment
- Population with access to local health care

In some cases, local, state, national, and international education and other agencies may want to consider illustrative indexes to collect, compare, and communicate significant data. Gordon's article "State of the Future Index (SOFI): A Method for Improving Decision Making That Affects the Future" (2003b) offers a good place to start.

Appendix D

A Sample Council Meeting Agenda

Determining Our Vision: What are the Characteristics of an Education System Capable of Preparing Students for a Global Knowledge/Information Age?

- **8:30 a.m. Social Time, Conversation, Continental Breakfast.**
- **9:00 a.m. A Brief Welcome.** The honorary chair welcomes everyone and makes brief, compelling remarks. Others, such as the superintendent, university or college president, or board chair, briefly but powerfully describe how the process will work and how it might affect the organization and its future.
- **9:10 a.m. A Briefing on Local, National, and International Issues and Trends.** This portion of the program should provide a glimpse of history, as well as current and developing political, economic, social, technological, environmental, and other forces affecting society and their possible implications for education in general and the organization in particular.
- **10:15 a.m. An Explanation of the Process.** A seasoned facilitator describes the process that will be used to generate thinking among council members. For example, after the opening plenary session, participants will be assigned to small groups—perhaps five to eight people each, depending on the size of the total group. Their charge will be to "Identify the characteristics of a school or school system (or college or university) capable of preparing students for life in a global knowledge/information age."
- **10:30 a.m. Break.**

- **10:45 a.m. Engagement in the Small-Group Process: Identifying Characteristics.** Reconvene in designated small groups. Ideally, in addition to the plenary facilitator, astute and experienced facilitators and recorders will be assigned to each of these small groups. Facilitators and recorders, who are not members of the council, will ensure that everyone in the group participates, that the ideas are clear, and that each characteristic is recorded on a separate sheet of 8-1/2-by-11-inch paper for later consideration. Brainstorming techniques should be used to ensure productive thinking and to keep the group from identifying one characteristic and then discussing it to death. Each characteristic should be distinct, not a combination of two or more others, and each should be written as a short but complete sentence. While the recorder is writing each idea down on paper, perhaps even on separate PowerPoint slides, the facilitator might use a flip-chart pad to capture and refine each characteristic so that everyone in the group can see and contribute to the process.

- **12:00 p.m. Break, Possible Tour of Historic Venue and Lunch.** During this lunch break, recorders check the characteristics they've recorded on individual sheets of paper or print copies of PowerPoint slides. Either way, each item should be stated on a separate sheet.

- **1:15 p.m. Continuation of the Small-Group Process: Placing Characteristics in Categories, Developing Summary Statements.** Facilitators show members of the small groups each of the characteristics they have identified. Characteristics are presented one at a time. Members of the group then suggest how the individual items should fall within categories, based on their similarity. (A mat board works well for this process.) When the characteristics are sorted, grouped, and posted, members of the small group are asked to develop a basic description for each category, such as "instruction," "communication," and so on.

- **2:45 p.m. Break.** During this break, each small group sets up its display of characteristics by category for the upcoming plenary session.
- **3:05 p.m. Plenary Session: Sharing of Small-Group Work.** Each small group is given five to eight minutes to present its clusters of characteristics. When that process is complete, the plenary session facilitator asks the whole group to point out commonalities among the clusters of characteristics that have been identified. All of those individual characteristics are preserved and put to use in the follow-up process and in developing a final report or other type of publication.
- **4:20 p.m. Closing Remarks.** The honorary chair and perhaps an official of the organization express thanks, offer remarks about the historic significance of the effort, and explain the next steps in the process.

Appendix E

Examples of Partial Simulated Scenarios

Note: The data and situations come largely from real school systems, though the name Acme City Unified School District #88 is fictitious. The scenarios have been abbreviated and cover some, but not all, of the issues affecting the organization and its students. Actual projections of growth or decline would likely be included for a number of the items mentioned in the scenarios in general terms.

Background

Enrollments: The current K–12 enrollment of the Acme City Unified School District #88 stands at 55,300, an increase of only 2,635 students, or 0.5 percent, over the past 10 years. On average, enrollments statewide have increased by 8.5 percent during that same period. Data from the past three years have shown a slight increase, a reversal from earlier declines.

Demographics: Demographic makeups of both the community and the student body have changed significantly.

Race/Ethnicity of Students:

- Non-Hispanic white students dropped from 65 percent of total enrollment 10 years ago to 28 percent this school year.
- Hispanic student enrollment grew from 14 percent 10 years ago to 45 percent this school year.
- Enrollment of African American students was 10 percent 10 years ago and remains at 10 percent this school year.

- Asian student enrollment was 8 percent 10 years ago and remains at 8 percent this school year.
- Native American student enrollment was 3 percent 10 years ago and remains at 3 percent this school year.
- Overall, diversity further increased during the past 10 years. In the current school year, 6 percent of students were identified as part of groups "other than those listed above."
- In the past 10 years, 20 percent of students who entered the schools were immigrants with limited English and a variety of education deficits, which the schools have been somewhat successful in helping them overcome.
- Students' first languages include, but are not limited to, Spanish, Vietnamese, Cantonese, Cambodian (Khmer), Somali, Arabic, Bosnian, Korean, Filipino (Tagalog), Portuguese, and Japanese.

Economics and Mobility:

- A regional office of one major corporation and numerous small businesses closed or left the community four years ago. However, during the past two years, a major high-tech firm located its district office within the school district. Local newspapers have written recently about a growth in cottage industries.
- During the first 8 years of this 10-year period, numerous high- and medium-income families moved from the city to other communities. Many have left the city because of a statewide economic crisis that made other areas of the state and country more attractive for professional employment.
- During the past two years, gentrification has brought some high- to middle-income families back into the older areas of the city.

Families with School-Age Children: Approximately 75 percent of households in the district do not have children in the school system.

Educational Programs/Assessments:

- Average disaggregated test scores have shown modest increases for each racial/ethnic group during the past two years. Reading scores for the current year averaged five points below state averages. Math scores are four points below state averages.
- Despite educational and financial challenges, the school system now has some programs in place to work more effectively with immigrant students and their parents.
- Although the district has been diligent in developing programs to meet the needs of all students, many of those programs are idle because of a lack of funds.
- A new program in public and private entrepreneurship is expected to offer additional hope for current students. Some adult education classes are included. One of the program's purposes is to help provide an economic stimulus for the community within five years.
- A technology plan has been developed to enhance instruction and to prepare students for entry-level jobs, but implementation is two years behind schedule because of a lack of funding.
- Concern has grown that standards and requirements imposed by state and federal governments, coupled with high-stakes tests, may emphasize failure rather than recognize the heroic efforts of school district staff, leadership, and involved parents.

Funding:

- The state has a law on the books limiting increases in annual school budgets. However, the law does include an override provision, which would require a public vote. If the override is approved, it could allow the district to modestly exceed the state-imposed limitation.
- After two failures four and five years ago, a recent bond to support building construction and renovation passed with a 60 percent "yes" vote. An analysis of those who voted indicated that 40 percent of

longer-term, middle- to upper-income residents voted "yes" in the most recent election. However, 70 percent of first- and second-generation immigrants and lower-income residents voted "yes," which ensured passage.

- During the past 10 years, the state's portion of the school district budget has increased from 25 to 45 percent. However, the state's tax revenues have been hit by an economic downturn, which, in turn, has limited the district's ability to amass the funds it needs to meet growing challenges.
- Basic costs of running the school system have gone up an average of 2 percent during each of the past three years, but funding has only gone up 1 percent a year, leading to substantial cuts in staffing and programs.

Scenarios

Based on this background information, the following three scenarios have been developed. All are based on *five-year projections of alternative futures*. (One is presented with bullets and two in paragraph form to illustrate possible differences in formats. In actual use, scenario titles would likely be more subtle.)

Scenario: A Glimmer at the End of the Tunnel

Within five years, it is anticipated that

- Enrollments will increase by a total of 3 percent.
- Racial/ethnic makeup of the population will stabilize at about its present level.
- A tax override vote will pass, which will allow the district to increase its budget up to 2 percent a year for the next three years.
- Education programs designed to help all students achieve somewhat higher levels of academic success will be more adequately funded.

Reading and math scores are expected to be at or above state averages within five years.

- First- and second-generation immigrant families will continue to climb the economic ladder, based on their belief that education is the key to a better future. Growing numbers of students from these families will enter community colleges as well as four-year colleges and universities. When they complete their formal education, they will pursue entrepreneurial activities, and 50 percent of that group will remain as contributing, taxpaying members of the community.

- With gentrification, increasing numbers of middle- and high-income families, many with few or no children, will move back into the older parts of the city during the next five years.

Scenario: The Headlamp of an Oncoming Train

During the next five years, this scenario anticipates defeat of a tax override; a worsening of the state's economy, leading to even more drastic cuts in financial support; an increase in immigrant populations, requiring additional programs to address language and other adjustment needs; a declining enrollment; an accelerated move of businesses and middle- and high-income people out of the city; and a continued demand that students meet state and federal standards.

Scenario: Sunlight at the End of the Tunnel

During the next five years, the school system anticipates the following events and developments: passage of a tax-limitation override, allowing more substantial increases in the system's budget; a burgeoning state economy, leading to even greater levels of state financial support; first- and second-generation immigrants pursuing education opportunities that lead to better jobs and the creation of new businesses; an accelerated move back into the city by middle- and high-income people who had previously moved out; the ability of the community to attract industries that will provide hundreds of jobs and boost the citywide economy; and higher levels of achievement by students, leading to a positive community attitude and even further success.

References

Adams, A. E. (2003, Summer). [Review of the book *Collective behavior and public opinion: Rapid shifts in opinion and communication*, by Jaap van Ginneken]. *American Communication Journal*, 6(4).

Alternative Futures. (2003, December). Intriguing ideas. Alexandria, VA: Institute for Alternative Futures. Available: http://www.altfutures.com/news/Dec%2003%20Alternative%20Futures.pdf

American Association of Retired Persons and Administration on Aging, U.S. Department of Health and Human Services. (1999). *A profile of older Americans 1999*. Washington, DC: Author.

Axelrod, A. (2000). *Elizabeth I, CEO: Strategic lessons from the leader who built an empire*. Paramus, NJ: Prentice-Hall.

Bagin, D., Ferguson, D., & Marx, G. (1985). *Public relations for administrators*. Arlington, VA: American Association of School Administrators.

Bagin, D., & Gallagher, D. R. (2001). *The school and community relations*. Needham Heights, MA: Allyn and Bacon.

Beaty, B. (2004). Other Feynman quotes. *The Feynman Webring*. Available: http://www.amasci .com/feynman.html

Bennis, W. (2002). Becoming a leader of leaders. In R. Gibson (Ed.), *Rethinking the future* (pp. 148–163). London: Nicholas Brealey Publishing.

Bennis, W., & Goldsmith, J. (2003). *Learning to lead: A workbook on becoming a leader* (3rd ed.). New York: Basic Books.

Bezold, C., Rhea, M., & Rowley, W. (2003, July 18). *Wiser futures*. Address presented at the pre-conference program, World Future Society annual conference, San Francisco.

Borawski, P., & Ward, A. (2004, Winter). Living strategy: Guiding your association through the rugged landscape ahead. *Journal of Association Leadership*, 2(1), 6–23.

Burtless, G. (1997, September). Social Security's long-term budget outlook. *National Tax Journal*, 50(3).

Chase, W. H. (1981). Issues management. In J. S. Nagelschmidt (Ed.), *The public affairs handbook* (pp. 104–105). New York: American Management Association (AMACOM).

Chase, W. H. (1984). *Issue management: Origins of the future*. Stamford, CT: Issue Action Publications.

Cleveland, H. (2002a). *Nobody in charge: Essays on the future of leadership*. San Francisco: Jossey-Bass.

Cleveland, H. (2002b, September–October). Leadership: The get-it-all-together profession. *The Futurist*, 36(6), 42–47.

Coates, J. (2002, July 19–20). *How to think like a futurist*. Presentation at the pre-conference program of the World Future Society, Philadelphia.

Cornish, E. (2004). *Futuring: The exploration of the future*. Bethesda, MD: World Future Society.

Cutlip, S., Center, A., & Broom, G. (1994). *Effective public relations.* Englewood Cliffs, NJ: Prentice-Hall.

Delcore, D. (2002, October 13). Williamstown residents work on blueprint for school future. *Times Argus,* Montpelier, VT.

Dylan, B. (1964). The times they are a-changin'. On *The times they are a-changin'* [CD]. Los Angeles: Columbia Records.

Education Commission of the States (ECS). (1999). *Future trends affecting education.* Available: http://www.ecs.org/clearinghouse/13/27/1327.htm

Education Commission of the States (ECS). (2003). *Education issues.* Available: http://www.ecs.org

Florida, R. (2004). *The rise of the creative class.* New York: Basic Books.

FOLIO (Facilitated Online Learning as an Interactive Opportunity). (2004, June). *Managing change for health information professionals (MCHIP).* Available: http://www.nelh.nhs.uk/folio/mchip/briefing2.htm

Fuller, R. B. (1969). *Operating manual for spaceship Earth.* Carbondale, IL: Southern Illinois University Press.

Gardner, H. (1993). *Multiple intelligences: The theory in practice.* New York: Basic Books.

Gelb, M. J. (1998). *How to think like Leonardo da Vinci.* New York: Dell Publishing.

Gibson, R. (Ed.). (2002). *Rethinking the future.* London: Nicholas Brealey Publishing.

Gladwell, M. (2002). *The tipping point: How little things can make a big difference.* Boston: Back Bay Books.

Godet, M. (2001). *Creating futures: Scenario planning as a management tool.* London: Economica Ltd.

Goodstein, D. (2004). *Out of gas: The end of the age of oil.* New York: W. W. Norton.

Gordon, T. J. (2003a, July 21). Presentation at the professional members' forum of the World Future Society, San Francisco.

Gordon, T. J. (2003b, Summer). State of the future index (SOFI): A method for improving decision making that affects the future. *Futures Research Quarterly, 19*(2), 5–11.

Grossman, L. (1998). Presentation at a conference of the World Future Society, Chicago.

Grunig, J. E., & Hunt, T. (1984). *Managing public relations.* New York: CBS College Publishing.

Hoyt, B. R. (2003, July 20). *The future of organizational structure.* Address presented at the annual conference of the World Future Society, San Francisco.

Issue Management Council. (n.d.). *The W. Howard Chase Award.* Available: http://www.issuemanagement.org/documents/chase.html

Kerr, M. (2001, November). *The Delphi process.* Retrieved January 9, 2004, from http://www.rararbids.org.uk/documents/bid79-delphi.htm

Kotter, J. (2002). Cultures and coalitions. In R. Gibson (Ed.), *Rethinking the future* (164–178). London: Nicholas Brealey Publishing.

Madsen, G., & Rosen, B. (1994, April). *Facilitative leadership: Tapping the power of participation.* Presentation at the annual conference of the American Association of School Administrators, New Orleans, LA.

Manktelow, J. (2005). SWOT analysis: Understanding strengths, weaknesses, opportunities, and threats. *MindTools: Essential Skills for an Excellent Career.* Available: http://www.mindtools.com/pages/article/newTMC_05.htm

Marx, G. (2000). *Ten trends: Educating children for a profoundly different future.* Arlington, VA: Educational Research Service.

Marx, G. (2001). Getting ready for a crisis. In D. Bagin & D. Gallagher (Eds.), *The school and community relations* (pp. 158–170). Needham Heights, MA: Allyn and Bacon.

Marx, G., & Educational Research Service. (2005). *16 trends: Their profound impact on our future*. Arlington, VA: Educational Research Service.

McNamara, C. (2005). *Basics of conducting focus groups*. Available: http://www.mapnp.org/library/evaluatn/focusgrp.htm

Meredith, G. E., & Schewe, C. D., with Karlovich, J. (2002). *Defining markets, defining moments*. New York: Hungry Minds.

Merriman-Clarke, K. (2001). Nobel laureates explore leadership in the new millennium. *Executive Update Online*, Greater Washington Society of Association Executives. Available: http://www.gwsae.org/executiveupdate/2001/september/electronicissue/leadership.htm

Morrison, J. L., & Wilson, I. (1997). Analyzing environments and developing scenarios in uncertain times. In M. W. Peterson, D. D. Dill, L. A. Mets, & Associates (Eds.), *Planning and management for a changing environment*. San Francisco: Jossey-Bass. Available: http://www.horizon.unc.edu/courses/papers/JBChapter.asp

Nagelschmidt, J. S. (Ed.). (1981). *The public affairs handbook*. New York: American Management Association (AMACOM).

Nair, K. (1994). *A higher standard of leadership: Lessons from the life of Gandhi*. Emeryville, CA: Berrett-Koehler.

Naperville Community Unit School District 203. (2004, September). *Strategic plan, 2004–05* [Brochure]. Naperville, IL: Author.

Paine, T. (1776). Thoughts on the present state of American affairs. *Common Sense*. Available: http://www.bartleby.com/133/3.html

Petersen, J. L. (1999). *Out of the blue: How to anticipate big future surprises*. Lanham, MD: Madison Books.

RAND Europe. (n.d.). *Scenarios*. Available: http://www.rand.org/randeurope/fields/scenarios.html

Ratcliffe, J. (2003, Winter). Scenario planning: An evaluation of practice. *Futures Research Quarterly, (19)*4, 5–25.

Rubenstein, H. (1999). *Breakthrough, Inc.: High growth strategies for entrepreneurial organizations*. London: Financial Times/Prentice-Hall.

Rubenstein, H. (2000, Fall). Strategic planning for futurists. *Futures Research Quarterly*.

Santosus, M. (1998, April 15). Simple, yet complex. *CIO Enterprise*. Available: www.cio.com

Schwahn, C. J., & Spady, W. G. (1998). *Total leaders: Applying the best future-focused change strategies to education*. Arlington, VA: American Association of School Administrators.

Schwartz, P. (1995). *The art of the long view*. New York: Currency Doubleday.

Senge, P. (2002). Rethinking control and complexity. In R. Gibson (Ed.), *Rethinking the future* (pp. 122–146). London: Nicholas Brealey Publishing.

Silberglitt, R., & Hove, A. (n.d.). *A scenario analysis*. RAND Corporation. Available: http://www.rand.org/scitech/stpi/Evision/Supplement/scenario.pdf

Smyre, R. (2004). *Core skills for transformational learning*. Unpublished manuscript.

Spady, W., & Schwahn, C. (2001, December). Leading when everyone goes back to zero. *Principal Leadership, (2)*1.

State of the world. [Annual publication]. Washington, DC: Worldwatch Institute.

Stone, S. J. (1999). A conversation with John Goodlad. *Childhood Education*, 264–268.

Strauss, W., & Howe, N. (1991). *Generations: The history of America's future, 1584–2069*. New York: William Morrow.

Surowiecki, J. (2004). *The wisdom of crowds*. New York: Doubleday.

Sussmuth, R. (1998). The future-capability of society. In F. Hesselbein, M. Goldsmith, R. Beckhard, & R. F. Schubert (Eds.), *The community of the future* (pp. 27–34). San Francisco: Jossey-Bass.

Sweeney, J. (1991). *Tips for improving school climate.* Arlington, VA: American Association of School Administrators.

U.S. Social Security Administration. (2000). *The 2000 annual report of the Board of Trustees of the Federal Old-Age and Survivors Insurance and Disability Trust Funds.* Washington, DC: Author.

Vital signs. [Annual publication]. Washington, DC: Worldwatch Institute.

Webster's new collegiate dictionary (11th ed.). (2004). Springfield, MA: Merriam-Webster, Inc.

Wilber, K. (1996/2000). *A brief history of everything.* Boston: Shambhala.

Wilson, E. O. (1998). *Consilience: The unity of knowledge.* New York: Knopf.

Winchester, S. (2004). *Krakatoa.* New York: HarperCollins.

Withrow, F. (with Long, H., & Marx, G.). (1999). *Preparing schools and school systems for the 21st century.* Arlington, VA: American Association of School Administrators.

World almanac and book of facts 2004. (2004). New York: World Almanac Books.

World Future Society. (2004, May–June). The art of foresight. [Special report]. *The Futurist.*

Wylie, F. W. (1977, November 15). *Public relations: A frontier profession.* Inaugural address presented at the 30th national conference of the Public Relations Society of America, San Diego, CA.

Zollo, P. (2004). *Getting wiser to teens: More insights into marketing to teenagers.* Ithaca, NY: New Strategist Publications.

Index

About the Author

Gary Marx, CAE, APR, is president of the Center for Public Outreach (CPO), in Vienna, Virginia, an organization he founded in 1998. CPO provides counsel on future-oriented leadership, communication, education, community, and democracy.

As a speaker, workshop leader, and consultant, Marx has worked with education, community, business, association, and government leaders at all levels on four continents and in all 50 of the United States. He has been called an "intellectual entrepreneur, who is constantly pursuing ideas" and a "deep generalist."

As a futurist, Marx has directed studies such as *Preparing Students for the 21st Century* (1996), *Preparing Schools and School Systems for the 21st Century* (1999), *Ten Trends: Educating Children for a Profoundly Different Future* (2000), and *16 Trends: Their Profound Impact on Our Future* (2005). He is the author of numerous books and articles. During his career, Marx has been a source for local, national, and international news media on issues affecting education and society.

Before launching the Center for Public Outreach, Gary Marx served for nearly 20 years as a senior executive for the American Association of School Administrators (AASA). He was a television and radio broadcaster before moving into education, serving as an administrator for the Westside Community Schools in Omaha and the Jefferson County Public Schools in Colorado.

Marx was presented the coveted President's Award by the National School Public Relations Association in 1999 and the Distinguished Service

Award by AASA in 2000. He is accredited by the National School Public Relations Association, the Public Relations Society of America, and the American Society of Association Executives, and is a professional member of the World Future Society.

Gary Marx resides in the Washington, DC, area and can be reached by phone, 703-938-8725, or e-mail, gmarxcpo@aol.com.